Mary Gilliatt's

COMPLETE ROOM BY ROOM

DECORATING GUIDE

Mary Gilliatt's
COMPLETE ROOM BY ROOM DECORATING GUIDE

Photographs by Andreas von Einsiedel

WATSON-GUPTILL PUBLICATIONS/NEW YORK

Senior Acquisitions Editor: Victoria Craven
Project Editor: Anne McNamara
Designed by Areta Buk/Thumb Print
Graphic production by Ellen Greene
Text set in 8.5-pt. Trade Gothic Light

Text copyright © 2003 by Mary Gilliatt
Photographs copyright © 2003 Andreas von Einsiedel

First published in 2003 by Watson-Guptill Publications,
a division of VNU Business Media, Inc.,
770 Broadway, New York, N.Y. 10003
www.watsonguptill.com

LIBRARY OF CONGRESS CATALOGING-IN-PUBLICATION DATA

Gilliatt, Mary.
    Mary Gilliatt's complete room by room decorating guide / by Mary Gilliatt ;
photography by Andreas von Einsiedel.
        p. cm.
Follow-up to: Mary Gilliatt's interior design course. 2001.
Includes index.
ISBN 0-8230-2970-0 (hardcover : alk. paper)
1. Interior decoration. I. Title: Room by room decorating guide. II.
Gilliatt, Mary. Mary Gilliatt's interior design course. III. Title.
    NK2110 .G488 2003
    747—dc21

                                                2002156446

First printing, 2003

1 2 3 4 5 6 7 8 9 / 09 08 07 06 05 04 03

Acknowledgements

There have been many people involved in this book, and I am so grateful to all of them.

Working with Watson-Guptill has been a true pleasure. Victoria Craven first wanted to do the book, and expedited everything with grace, enthusiasm, and not least, friendship. Anne McNamara has been a joy to work with on the text; Lee Wiggins a joy to work with on the publicity. Areta Buk's design is all that an author could hope for.

On the personal front, I want to thank Andreas von Einsiedel, my favorite photographer, and his assistant, Elisa Merlo, who dealt with all administration so efficiently. Good dear friends and family: Barbara Plumb and Virginia LoFaro Cooper in New York; Jim and Judy Lance and Tom and Sophie Gilliatt in Sydney; Christopher and Anne Cruice Goodall, Jan Kern and David Gough, Carmel and John Jones in London; and Kate Coughlan in Auckland had me to stay more often and with more generosity than even the best of friendship requires while I was working on the research and writing. And Inge Heckel of the excellent New York School of Interior Design and Karen Powell and José Cicerale of that fast-growing franchise, Décor and You, have been especially supportive.

I would especially like to thank all of the home owners, designers, and architects, without whose contributions and talents this book would not have been possible. (For a complete list of contributing designers, please refer to page 159.)

For Jude,
who has been my much valued friend through
thick and thin, kith and kin...
with love and gratitude

Contents

Introduction

BELOW: A spare and elegant room, overlooking the River Thames, with space for everything and everything in its place. Note how the colors of the casually slung throw in the foreground repeat— either by serendipity or design—the bowls and hydrangeas on the desktop and the upholstery of the chairs in the background.

OPPOSITE: This bedroom, set high up in the eaves of an ancient stone house, looks like a dramatic but comfortable version of a medieval room. The sumptuous black velvet bed curtains and upholstery, the cream silk curtain linings, the crisp white bed linens, all combine to set the mise-en-scène.

WHEREVER AND WHICHEVER WAY WE CHOOSE TO LIVE, most of us need ideas, inspiration, and starting points for our various rooms. The decoration of any room is made up of the sum of its various parts: lighting, flooring, walls, woodwork, trim, windows, storage, soft furnishings, furniture, art and objects—or objets d'art—flowers, plants, what you will, and, of course, details like hardware, fabric trims, and so on and so forth. A color scheme and budget has to be decided upon, a list of what is currently available and what has to be bought has to be drawn, and, above all, a decorating style that will suit both ourselves and our home must be considered. It is a great deal to think about and a responsibility to get right, because whatever we choose invariably has to last a long time.

Naturally, living styles vary enormously depending upon the type, size, and age of the house or apartment, the size and ages of the family (if any), the location, climate, and, not least, tastes and income. But generally, whatever our circumstances, we share much the same universal criteria. That is to say—and I've repeated this over and over in my various books like a mantra—most of us aspire to a comforting, comfortable, welcoming home that works well, looks good, and is as individual and pleasing as we can make it. As that rather severe seventeenth-century stricture of Francis Bacon puts it—although clearly lacking architectural sensitivity, let alone sensitivity to architects' egos—"Houses are built to live in, and not to look at. Therefore let use bee preferred before uniformitie, except where both may bee had." In my belief, it is definitely that "both"—use and uniformity—for which we should strive.

There are, of course, exceptions. Some people, notably those without families or other people's needs to consider, are able to put aesthetics before practicality and to be as cutting edge or as purist in a particular style, whether of the moment or of the past, as they can afford or dare to be. And it is these exceptions, either leaders or just determined followers of fashion, who provide the clearest signposts, so to speak, to the progression (or, in the case of some periods, regression) of design. For somehow or other, almost every decade has its recognizable look or *feel* as much in furniture, soft furnishings, accessories, art, and colors as it does in clothes.

Apart from giving general advice on the decoration and furnishing of each room in the home (which inevitably leads to some repetition), this book shows some of the most interesting rooms to be seen currently around the world, chosen for their ability to set off new trains of thought, as well as for their different approaches to climate. Some have been done with very little money and a great deal of ingenuity; some are classically beautiful, though often with a twist; others are idiosyncratic. There are rooms that have an eye to the past, while others look to the future; many of the rooms mix the two. Regardless of their style, all of the rooms are in some way inspiring for the way we live now.

Starting Points

WE ARE FORTUNATE AT THIS TIME TO HAVE SO MANY
decorating styles to choose from and to adapt to our own and our
home's requirements. While ways of living have changed down
the decades, with new materials and new habits, there is yet no
question that some knowledge of the styles of the past helps us
to better understand the choices available today.

Documenting Styles

AT THIS TIME, WITH SO MUCH INTEREST IN THE HOME, the decorating options appear endless, as does as the selection of merchandise available from almost every part of the world. This can be good only as long as the notion of such enormous choice does not overwhelm us. Looking back over centuries of domestic looks gives an idea of the exhaustive choice of styles available and furthers one's understanding of the cyclical nature of interior design. In any case, I am a great believer that we need to know something about the past in order to understand the present, let alone the future.

Tastes cannot help but change down the decades and the generations with new materials and habits. Most of us live much more casually today than did our forbears. We also have some new rooms. The so-called "great rooms," media rooms, and home offices were rarely in existence even thirty years ago. But then we generally no longer possess boudoirs, ballrooms, or even night and day nurseries.

For anyone considering decorating or redecorating an entire home or even just one room, you can rarely look at enough good ideas and possible juxtapositions of furnishing ingredients, especially if you can put them in context with some knowledge of past styles. Today we have vast resources of interior photography and a proliferation of decorating magazines, books, and television programs to inform us about current designs, but in the late eighteenth and early nineteenth centuries, before the advent of interior photography, rooms were recorded primarily in amateur watercolors. Before that, it was possible to discern contemporary interior styles and colors in the backgrounds of portraits and genre paintings, where the richness of color and detailing is often astounding.

All of these aids have helped our appreciation of the history of taste, and certainly have given us more knowledge than our ancestors could ever have had. Photography especially

The grouping of the bust under the crystal chandelier and the Roman and early glass on the shallow brackets is certainly reminiscent of some of the spoils brought back by the fortunate recipients of the eighteenth-century "Grand Tours." The muted amber colors look good against the gently paneled walls.

has made an enormous difference to the records, given the fact that so many rooms get destroyed as people move on, or are altered in feeling over the years as their occupants try out new schemes.

It is possible to get an excellent idea of the architectural details, decoration, furnishings, and colors current in various periods from the beautifully detailed rooms set up in museums, like the Metropolitan Museum of Art in New York, the Victoria & Albert and the Jeffreye Museums in London, and the Musée des Arts Décoratifs in Paris. Yet it is often hard, since they have never actually been lived in, to instill much sense of everyday life into these period rooms. If one visits stately homes and old country mansions, which are open to the public in various countries, one can get a good feel for the appurtenances of daily living down the decades, even if it was rather grand living, as well as the architecture, scale, and proportions of the relevant period. But it is really very rare for a house to be decorated all of a piece when it is first built and then left untouched. Usually such houses have been lived in by many generations of the same family, so that their rooms are more monuments to the accretions of various progeny. They are therefore more like "normal" rooms in that they are exercises in eclecticism, albeit an unconscious, ongoing, and layered eclecticism.

The First International Styles

Interior decorating styles became more or less international from the late 1780s Neo-Classical period onwards. This was due mainly to the general increase in travel, whether those travelers were members of the aristocracy doing their "Grand Tours," diplomats, soldiers back from the various wars, merchant traders, adventurers, or just intrepid voyagers. Drawings and paintings of classical architecture from Greece and Italy; sculpture, furniture, and paintings of Egypt and India; the sudden interest in Egyptology as a result of the Napoleonic Campaigns; even the stripes of the soldiers' tents, swords, and spear heads, were all absorbed into the vocabulary of current decoration.

Various emblems from ancient Greece, like acanthus leaves, amphora (a Greek vase form with two handles and a narrow neck), anthemion (conventionalized honeysuckle or palm leaves), and Greek key designs, appeared as moldings, borders, and as decorative motifs on furniture. From Egypt came more motifs like sphinxes, winged lions, lion heads and legs (the rear legs used for the back legs of chairs, the forelegs for the fronts), swan and duck heads, cobras, griffins, and vultures. Motifs from ancient Rome included torches, winged Victories, caryatids, sacrificial scenes, dancing girls, heads of the gods like Bacchus, Hermes, and Apollo, rams' and horses' heads, laurel wreaths, masks, military and musical instruments, swords and lances, and more griffins and swans.

Communications, too, were greatly improved, and various fashions were frequently described in letters, many of which have been preserved. Moreover, the best European furniture designers and makers were beginning to distribute their pattern books across the Atlantic, just as porcelain, fabric, and wallpaper manufacturers were distributing their wares internationally, from East to West and from Europe to the Americas.

The stripes of the soldiers' tents in the Napoleonic Campaigns introduced the Neo-Classical fashion for striped and often "tented" rooms. Note the classical motif above the window to the rear and the mural of the banks of the Nile on the side wall.

The Scandinavian stove, together with the striped upholstered beds and the continuous broad blue band running at dado height around the room and around the doors and windows, gives a Swedish Gustavian feel to this room. "Gustavian" is the name given to the late-eighteenth-century simplified form of Neo-Classicism in Sweden, called after the late King Gustav III, who popularized the style.

Shared Facets

Most of so-called Western civilization (including the Antipodes and South Africa, with colonial off-shoots in the East, East and West Indies, and India) shared many of the varied facets of the nineteenth century. For example, the Neo-Classical style was followed at the turn of the century by the much heavier and more solemn Empire style in France (full of allusions to Rome's Imperial splendor, and therefore considered only fitting for the Emperor Napoleon). The lighter Regency style in Britain ran more or less parallel to the Empire style, with many of the same classical and Egyptian allusions, plus the remarkable Hindu influence, to be seen at its apotheosis of fantasy in the Prince Regent's Pavilion in Brighton.

At much the same time, the impressive Federal, Greek Revival, and American Empire styles ran their course in the United States. Biedermeier in Austria and Scandinavia was

considered to be the poor man's Empire, but was none the worse for that. And most other countries followed variations of these styles. Alas, after the almost universal elegance and restraint of the Neo-Classical and early Regency, Federal, and Greek Revival periods, things began to tail off in the late Regency and American Empire periods. Then, almost everyone shared the general eclecticism and revivalism that took place from around 1840 till near the end of the century, as the machine and its partner, mass production, took hold.

There were various attempts to push back, or rise above, this flood of mass reproductions. The Arts and Crafts Movement that began in the 1860s in Britain, under the aegis of William Morris, questioned how the machine should best be used and preached a return to honest craftsmanship and the inclusion of art and design in everyday life. ("Have nothing in your house that you do not know to be useful and think to be beautiful," he wrote later in the essay, "The Beauty of Life," 1880.) The movement was soon taken up in the United States, as was the Queen Anne Revival in the 1870s, interspersed with the Aesthetic Movement of the 1880s, and followed by the Art Nouveau Movement, which ran through the turn of the century.

Art Nouveau, with its asymmetrical, amazingly vegetal style, was a conscious attempt to produce a wholly original look that owed absolutely nothing to the past. It started in Belgium with designers like Henri van der Velde and Victor Horta, and swept right through Europe and America with designers like Hector Guimard, Emile Gallé, and Eugene Gaillard in France, Antonio Gaudi in Spain, Peter Behrens in Germany, Carlo Bugatti in Italy, Charles Rennie Mackintosh in Great Britain, and Louis Comfort Tiffany in the United States, all of them working on their own variations. But this "art for art's sake" style, which, at its most florid was almost entirely decorative, ran alongside the Queen Anne Revival, the "sweetness and light" Edwardian movement, *and* the Rococo and Renaissance Revivals. These last three somewhat regressive styles, or a mixture thereof, seemed to be the look of choice for many major industrialists, press barons, merchants, and traders in the period of huge prosperity that ran from the last part of the nineteenth century until the beginning of the First World War in 1914.

TOP RIGHT: In this room, renditions of a Regency chaise lounge and chair, and a graceful piece of Biedermeier furniture are set next to a marble fireplace.

RIGHT: A nice grouping of a Roman bust set atop a Tuscan column next to an urn and an American early-nineteenth-century chair in a paneled room.

The Origins of Modernism

ALSO AT THE RESTLESS TURN OF THE CENTURY, rather more radical modernist movements were evolving in Austria, Germany, and the United States. Members of the Vienna Wiener Werkstaette, like Josef Hoffman, Adolf Loos (of "Ornament = Crime" fame), Dagobert Peche, Koloman Moser, and Otto Wagner, were designing what they hoped would be truly classic furniture, objects, and buildings for the twentieth century, which they certainly turned out to be. In Germany, the Deutscher Werkbund in Dresden and the Vereinigte Werkstatten in Munich were combining straight lines with curves to create designs that had a much lighter feeling than their predecessors. In the United States, the brothers Charles and Henry Greene in California and Frank Lloyd Wright in Chicago were also creating more sleek, geometric styles.

The two, quite opposite, movements of the Bauhaus and Art Deco, or Art Moderne as it was known in America—the one so spare and totally unlike anything else that had been before, the other so decorative, even sumptuous—ran concurrently more or less from 1918, with various adaptations until the 1930s. The Second World War, from 1939–45, created all sorts of new furniture and furnishing materials as the result of wartime research, particularly that on airplane manufacturing. After the war, the resumption of the tenets of the Bauhaus Movement resulted in the International Style/Modern Movement of the 1940s and 50s (versions of which still pop up today). This was followed by the blazing colors and plastic forms of the 1960s, of which Italy was the master; the Plexiglas, glass, steel, hi-tech, and minimalism of the 1970s; and the newfound lushness and eclecticism of the 1980s. The 1990s-style minimalism continues to today, with a very pleasant, clean-cut, rather pared-down eclecticism that is comparatively easy to effect. It combines both comfort and practicality, and, because it *is* so eclectic, does not look as if it will date.

LEFT: Colored Lucite chairs show up like oversized jewels on a limestone floor. The clean, minimalist design of the furniture and setting, the hi-tech materials, and crisp color scheme are all signature modernism.

OPPOSITE: A long strip of a shade in candy-button fabric is the focal point, at least for the eye, in this small living room. The 1930s-looking upholstery colors and cushions take their cue from it, while the floor and walls are kept light and white.

The Consumer Age

I mention all these styles of the last two hundred years at such a pace and in some detail to show the enormously varied fashions that took hold and eventually filtered down to the more general public. This happened with far greater rapidity with the improvements to printing and the consequent proliferation of magazines and newspapers. All this, as well as the ever-expanding mass-production and inevitable rise in general retailing, seems to have been as much a tragedy for good taste as it was a blessing for the less well-off.

Unhappily, what is high fashion today becomes all too easily tomorrow's leftovers. The numerous large retail stores and chains, and all of the mail-order catalogues that ceaselessly circle the globe, offer an endless source of new merchandise and new designs. Combined with the ability of manufacturers to reproduce or copy quickly, today's consumers are being almost overwhelmed by choices, not to mention the temptations provided by the staggering number of antique stores, markets, and emporiums found in cities and towns in a vast number of countries. The assiduous and informed shopper can now reproduce not only most period styles but also most national and regional styles of each country, should they so wish. "English Country" in Oregon and "Spanish Hacienda" in New Jersey, "Tuscan style" in Sydney, the "American South-West" in outer London, "Scandinavian Modern" in Paris, "Provence" in Holland, and "Greece" in Provence . . . there is no stopping it.

Of course, in many ways it is quite wonderful to have such a choice of merchandise in so many price ranges from so many countries. On the other hand, the roller-coaster turnover of fashions is, not unnaturally, somewhat unsettling, particularly for the assiduous fashion-follower. How restful, one may think, to have been living in ancient Egypt, where so little changed over the centuries and so few decisions regarding style had to be made.

It is only sensible therefore—unless one has generous amounts of money, time, patience, and the means to make constant changes—to use fashion as and when you find it desirable, rather than be dictated to, and sometimes tyrannized by it. This involves the ability to recognize the difference between ephemeral trends and newly interesting juxtapositions. The difference between, say, the over-use of the color purple with a lot of gilt and glitter and the use of natural fibers with brushed steel or nickel. In short, the difference between what is au courant and what might be a constant pleasure for years to come; the difference between good and bad design. But I should reiterate in all fairness, that if everyone tried to ignore fashion completely in order to pursue a timeless, classic look, or if everyone took a totally pragmatic and practical approach to decoration, there would never be any rooms available, whether recorded in photographs or somehow physically preserved, to bear witness to their time.

BELOW: Snowy white built-in stone benches make splendidly relaxed couches in the Greek Cypriot manner, with mattresses and scatter cushions covered in bright ethnic fabrics. The paintings on wood on the walls, the hanging pierced brass lamp, and the small octagonal table complete the look.

OPPOSITE: Lanterns, mirrors, lamps, and shades like this glowing collection can be bought quite easily thanks to the imagination of various importers.

Making Choices

ALL IN ALL THEN, THE CHOICES OF HOW BEST TO DECORATE seem to lie between the following alternatives: Firstly, you can try to suit furnishings and decorations to the particular style of the building, and/or to the environment or climate. Although in the case of a period house, this does not mean that you should follow the building's style absolutely slavishly. I would rather try for a sensitive interpretation within the spirit of the building and its surroundings. Quite apart from today's more casual living styles, there have been huge improvements in comforts like heating, air conditioning, lighting, and general plumbing, which our ancestors would most surely have taken advantage of, if they could have done so.

Another approach is to be cutting-edge contemporary, whatever contemporary happens to be at the time, and to go temporarily with the flow (because it *will* be temporary unless you are of the mind to turn your rooms into a monument to a particular time and period, or have decided not to spend any more money on your home for the duration). This involves a good deal of self-confidence, a strong sense of current design *moeurs*, and, very possibly, a great deal of storage.

Brilliant red walls with a complicated stenciled border, an intricate tiled floor, and beautiful wrought iron shutters are a fitting background for the pair of regal inlaid chairs.

Again, whatever your building's style, you can opt to choose more or less classic anchor pieces—large upholstered sofas and armchairs, bookcases, storage pieces, armoires, and so on—pepped up with contemporary furniture and accessories, which can be changed or replaced at will.

Finally, you can be thoroughly eclectic and choose what suits you best from the enormous choice of styles, mixing antique with modern, fanciful with practical, serious pieces of furniture with the frivolous, and casual with formal.

The question of how exactly to make the best choice is, of course, a vexed one and not just because of the largesse available. When more than one person in a marriage, partnership, or family has to put forward their opinion, there has to be compromise, unless, by some extraordinary miracle, everybody feels the same or has perfect confidence in one nominated decision-maker. Then too, there is the question of budget, which very seldom seems to be enough to cover all needs. Happily, in decoration more than in most things, the necessity of compromise often turns out to be a blessing whether in combining disparate tastes or coming up with cheaper and often more ingenious alternatives. At best the results will be original and interesting; at worst, there will be an unattractive muddle, or the sort of unhappy blandness that happens when everyone tries to play it safe.

The twin beds in this charming room could well be Northern Italian or Spanish, as well as Scandinavian. Notice the bluish-lavender rugs, checked throws, and ribbons matching the edging around the room.

Gaining Confidence

Conversely, there are the many people who lack confidence in their own taste and judgment to such an extent that they admit to having no idea what to choose or where to begin. I have one simple and obvious solution for this that rarely seems to fail, and that is to buy or borrow as many decorating magazines and books as possible. Tear out all the pages of rooms in magazines that are appealing, and tag all of the book pages. Put them all aside for a week or two and then go back to them with a fresh mind. Almost invariably there will be common denominators of style, color, arrangement, or some other general factor, and these clearly will be the hitherto unrevealed preferences.

Having at least discovered their design predilections, the faint-hearted or inexperienced should then make a concerted effort to really see and take notice of everything to do with decoration and to analyze *why* they like or dislike something in merchandise, art, and objects as well as rooms that they happen to visit. Moreover, they should continue to collect photographs of what they like in order to give themselves a cache of ideas to sift through and play around with. Rather than deciding to duplicate existing ideas, they should experiment with using part of this idea with that—this kind of color scheme but that sort of furniture, this kind of art but with those interesting rugs. In other words, they should absorb as many different ideas as possible and then repeat them but in a different way. This should start to inject confidence in their taste in a very short time.

In fact, although I know this is common sense to the majority, I would reiterate that *everyone* thinking of decorating or redecorating a room should collect a mass of cuttings, as well as samples of paint colors, fabrics, papers, borders, and various textures. Juggle them around and place them in different juxtapositions working out what would be best to use for what (for example, wall colors, trim, floor coverings, window treatments, and upholstery). Don't forget those items that you already possess that can be dyed, painted, re-covered, or otherwise updated. Whittle down and categorize until you are very sure that these are the final schemes that you can live with quite happily.

This collection of blue-and-white pots and jars looks fresh and decorative bursting with brightly colored tulips, especially with the painting of blue-and-white porcelain as a backdrop.

First Things First

Here is a list of simple precautions that will save you both aggravation and expense:

- Before you start decorating, make sure that the framework of each room is right. That is to say, decide if there could be any structural improvements that might make a difference to its scale, proportion, and space.
- Be sure that all lighting and power needs (including computers, phones, TVs, stereos, and appliances) are planned for and executed before any decorating is started.
- Draw out rough scale plans on graph paper for each of your rooms, marking in doorways, radiators, windows, and each of their measurements (height and width), as well as the measurements of front doors, turns in stairs, and elevators. Decide what you want lit and by what means, and mark in where you want outlets.
- Note measurements of furniture that you already have. Measure the repeats of patterned fabric, wallpaper, or carpet that you would like to use, to work out how much of each you will need.
- When shopping for furniture, take along your scale plans and a tape measure. Measure everything that you would like to buy and make sure that it will fit through the front door of your building as well as into the relevant rooms, and that it will also go up the stairs or into the building's elevator.

The charm of this basically white bedroom lies in its simplicity. It is a restful and comfortable room that will stay looking good for years. The bed curtains are exactly the same as those for the windows. The bedspread with its scalloped edges and the head-board with its shirred edging are nice, gentle details.

Halls, Staircases, and Landings

THE ENTRANCE HALL OR HALLWAYS CREATE THE first and last impression of a home, while staircases, corridors, and landings connect the various rooms. With a little time and thought, these often neglected areas can be decorated to significantly enhance a home's overall charm and appeal.

Making Connections

THE ENTRANCE HALL WELCOMES VISITORS TO OUR HOME and tickles the appetite, as it were, for the pleasures beyond. For many centuries, before the advent of any sense of true comfort, not to say security, and the consequent need for more relaxing sitting rooms, it was the most important room in any large house. Almost all of the general living and a great deal of the sleeping went on there. Even as late as the eighteenth century, Isaac Ware in "A Complete Body of Architecture" (1756), wrote that "a hall must be large and noble since it serves as the Summer room for dining; it is an ante-chamber in which people of business or of the second rank wait and amuse themselves, and it is a good apartment for the reception of large companies..."

Yet now it is all too often the last, not the first, area to be considered, the poor relation to all the other rooms, and all too often the catch-all for the household detritus like unopened mail, unwanted publicity literature, sporting paraphernalia, children's strollers and toys, and goodness knows what else. This is not to say that there should not be signs of regular life. Umbrellas, walking sticks, dog leads, and outdoor coats are

If a corridor is wide enough to take a table or another piece of furniture it should have it, for it is these connecting points that add extra character and usefulness to a home. Here, a pretty grouping of side table, mirror, lamps, and flowers is framed by a handsomely arched door opening. The large wall bracket to the side holds an equally handsome old Chinese ginger jar.

LEFT: One does not often have this kind of space for a landing, but if it exists it could certainly be used in a similar way as this. The daybed stretched at an angle under the Palladian window looks like an excellent and comfortable place for a relaxed read. It has the requisite angled light behind it, as well as a good chest on the side for dumping books and papers. The coir matting is topped with a colorful rug, which is matched in tones by the throw on the chaise.

BELOW: This is a staircase with attitude: a dual-purpose display area and floor connection all in one. The heads and bits of Oceanic sculpture planted on each stair leave sufficient room for the passerby while showcasing the collection. There are no banisters, simply an insouciant glass ball with drawings and paintings placed judiciously on the wall behind.

after all the natural extra ingredients in such a space when there is no good old-fashioned "back hall" in existence. Nonetheless, any entrance hall should be well-tended, reasonably tidy, cheerful, and welcoming, and not just a convenient dumping place.

Staircases, corridors, and landings, the connecting points to the various living areas, are also often treated rather summarily, although with a little forethought they could provide much needed extra storage space, or space for art and books, or even the odd desk, chair, and lamp. In fact, with a little care, these areas can greatly add to the charm and the general ambiance of a home.

Of course, it seems only logical when forming a decorating budget to allow the most money for rooms you are actually going to live in (although if the hall is big enough, particularly in an apartment, the space can often be used as a dining room, library, study or home office). But once these seemingly more pressing priorities have been decided, you should turn considerable thought to making the entrance to your home as agreeable as possible. It might come last on your list of necessities, but there is no real need for it to look the least important. In any case, given their generally modest dimensions, most existing halls should be comparatively inexpensive to design and furnish, unless you happen to be blessed with a particularly large area. Even then, my own opinion is that you will need little in the way of furniture since Mies van der Rohe's dictum that "Less is more," applies especially, I think, to entryways, where a sense of space can often give the illusion, not quickly dispelled, that the home is spacious in general.

Airy Versus Overstuffed

I emphasize my own opinion because of a sense of aggrievement I still hold, somewhat absurdly, over an incident at a decorators' showcase in a run-down, chateau-like house in the Hamptons, Long Island, New York. Many years ago, I was asked to decorate the airy, well-proportioned, and clearly, formerly elegant hall. I wanted to exaggerate or at least bring out these intrinsic qualities and concentrated my efforts and budget on putting down a beautiful inlaid limestone floor. I also hired a decorative painter to work on an exquisite faux marble–paneled dado below a newly installed chair rail, with gentle rag rolling above and a lovely French Rococo-styled painted ceiling.

I then installed a rather rare chandelier, spare but graceful painted shutters, found a splendid round table for the center, a good-looking and rather elaborate nineteenth-century bench, a pair of Louis XVI chairs, and brought in large specimen indoor trees in Versailles pots with carefully placed up-lights beneath, as well as a few good borrowed paintings. I was agreeably pleased with the result, and so was shocked, not to mention

This magnificent hall space lends itself to a kind of deliberately casual, throw-away decoration. Blue console tables placed on either side of the fireplace are teamed with a pair of blue-painted iron chairs. Long, colored-glass oil lamps hang before the chimneypiece, although it is mainly the chandelier that lights the space.

hurt, to be telephoned by a representative of the committee who said she felt that I had let them all down by the evident paucity of my effort. Why, I wanted to know, was that? "Well," was the answer, "we expected many more *things*. Surely there should be much more *stuff*. We want it to look rich, *rich, rich*." Leaving aside our obvious differences on the definition of richness, I argued that I simply did not agree and that in any house I was decorating with a hall of similar size and proportions, whether for clients or for myself, I would have done much the same thing, so why do anything different for a show house.

They were not appeased and even threatened, somewhat hysterically, to sue unless I brought in more furniture and accessories. This was evident nonsense, but nonetheless deeply unpleasant. In any event, I really could not think of what else I could possibly add without making the space seem somewhat overcrowded. As far as I can recall, I imported a few books and some flowers for the table, and in the end, it all blew over. Obviously, this was merely a question of style and taste. And taste, as we all know, is highly subjective. Who, after all, is to be the arbiter? It is easy to take a lawyer's opinion on a point of law, a doctor's opinion on a medical matter, an accountant's opinion on tax issues . . . but anything to do with design and decoration is often perceived as a kind of free-for-all.

Leaving the questions of taste, style, and suitability aside, the fact remains that whatever the size of a hall, whatever the budget, you will still need to plan for convenience as well as impact; for wear and tear as well as effect; and for physical warmth in a cool climate and coolness in a hot climate, since feel and comfort are quite as important as looks. In fact, without a sense of physical comfort and ease it is quite impossible to properly enjoy any interesting decorative effect, however stunning.

Decorative Options

One of the many advantages of immersing ourselves in the history of interior design is that we develop a sensitivity to scale and architectural detail. Such insight is helpful when trying to improve areas such as halls and corridors. Before decorating, always consider first the framework of the area, such as the walls and doors, and determine how best to present and utilize the space that is available.

Walls

Walls in halls and entranceways can be altered to expand the space or to add different views to adjacent living areas. If walls in a smallish hall are of the partition rather than structural variety, you could alter them a little to make the given space seem more generous. For example, in a townhouse, apartment, or any house where the front door opens directly into a small hall or corridor-like vestibule,

you could cut out a large square or arched opening instead of a conventional door going into the living room, or whatever room happens to open off the hall (unless it is a bedroom).

Alternatively, if the wall is long enough, you can make a squared opening with a pair of "windows" on either side to give different perspectives to the room ahead or on the side. Insert recessed down-lights into the top of these internal windows to light anything that you might care to place on the sills—plants perhaps, or interesting urns or vases—and you will instantly dramatize the space as well as exaggerate its size. The architect, Randy Croxton, who I had help me with my first rather dark apartment in New York, suggested this last idea and it made a profound difference, since I benefited instantly from the extra light from the living room windows. I have also seen people take a living room wall down to seating level, literally making a ledge for sitting. This way you will get all the benefit of extra light and

feeling of space and still have a division from the entryway. Another possibility is to cut narrow floor-to-ceiling slits in the wall. This will again offer interesting slithers of view into the adjacent room, as well as open up the given space.

In terms of possible wall treatments, options include paint, wallpaper, fabric, tile, and mirror. Whatever wall treatment you choose, be sure it as tough and durable as possible. Apart from needing to withstand the scrapes, fingerprints, and buffeting of human traffic and whatever it happens to be carrying, it is both expensive and a nuisance to have to redecorate, particularly where staircases, landings, and corridors are concerned. These areas generally need much the same treatment as the hall, unless they are in different parts of the home and cannot be seen one from another.

Since the walls of all the above areas lend themselves well to any number of pictures and memorabilia, and since they, on the whole, are inclined to be somewhat gloomy, often lacking a window, a solid dark or at least warmly colored paint makes a good background. So many people make the mistake of trying to lighten a space with white or a light color, which only ends up looking rather dreary. Any one of the gamut of reds makes a cheerful entrance, as do apricots, warm yellows, sands, and terra-cottas.

If ceilings are reasonably high, a chair or dado rail can divide the space. This is easily achieved by applying a run of molding about a third of the way up the wall from the floor, with a darker tone of the same color or a contrasting color painted in the space beneath. Wallpaper borders can be used on top of the paint, or wallpaper can be used over or under the chair or dado rail. For that matter, whole panels of wallpaper can be stuck over the paint and edged with either slim strips of molding or paper borders. This is good for making an expensive wallpaper go much further.

Any one of these ideas will add to the general interest of the space. However, given the rough treatment that entry and staircase walls tend to get, it is often advisable, especially if there are children, to coat all of the walls with clear matte or eggshell varnish. The varnish will both harden the surface and make it easier to clean. Likewise, there are dozens of other beguiling finishes and effects that look good and are practical for these areas—raised paneling, slabs of stone, old tiles, stencils, murals, polished lacquers, painted moldings and borders—its all a question of taste and budget. Whatever the choice though, remember the top layer of varnish or lacquer. This top coating is something I invariably apply to wallpapers as well, even if the paper is vinyl coated.

Doors

It is an axiom in architecture that if you can line up doors to open up vistas into other rooms you are injecting a real sense of anticipation and pleasure as well as providing a sense of order. It is certainly worth examining any doors opening off hallways and landings to see if they could be moved this way or that to make better visual sense.

On a more cosmetic note, doors in the same space should ideally be of the same size, wood, or color, with the same hardware. If the doors are not particularly handsome, they can always be exchanged for better ones with better hardware. Similarly, walls with no architectural detail can have cornices and various moldings added, as perhaps, a chair rail.

A pair of massive carved front doors are balanced by similarly proportioned and detailed doors at the back of the hall. The huge olive jar ensconced in the arched recess between the two is much the color of the limestone floor and perfectly proportioned both for the arch of the recess and the doors.

OPPOSITE: Walls with no particular architectural details can simply have details added if they suit the proportion and style of the building. It is quite easy to install cornices and chair rails like these in this interestingly shaped hall. The radiator cover makes a useful shelf, and the warm yellow of the walls is a good contrast to the black and gray of the tiles.

Fabric, although considerably more expensive than paint and most wallpapers, is long-lasting (sometimes for several decades), tough, and usually attractive, even sumptuous. Applications range from paper-backed burlap or felt in a variety of subtle to singing colors, to paper-backed suedes and faux suedes, which can be pasted straight to walls like papers. Then there are the silky suedes, leathers, printed or woven cottons, linens, damasks, corduroys, and velvets, which can be seamed and stretched over thin battens of wood which has been previously padded with a lining material known in the trade as "bump."

Many Mediterranean and Latin American houses have highly decorative ceramic tiled halls and stairwells that have a cooling effect, as of course have marble, lime, and sandstone. This is an expensive treatment but it can last forever and always looks good in hot climates. In cooler areas, leather tiles can look richly warm, polished like lovingly-tended old riding boots. Leather hangings were a much used decoration in the seventeenth and early eighteenth centuries in Europe.

Mirror can be valuable in a small hall or corridor, or as an exaggerator of the given space in a larger area. Walls can be lined in mirror in a narrow space, as can the ceiling for that matter, though this can play disorienting tricks with reflection. Mirror on a side wall in a hall or on the end wall of a corridor can totally change the look and feel of a space, especially if the wall happens to abut a window. Panels with mirror inserted in the center look glamorous at night and stretch the light by day. Even one oversized mirror will make a difference, as will a wall of differently shaped mirrors that reflect and refract light.

TOP LEFT: A baseboard to ceiling arched mirrored recess more than doubles the apparent width of a narrow hallway. Decorative painted panels on the terra-cotta walls are edged with the same color as the green dado beneath the chair rail, which in turn picks up the tone of the floor.

BOTTOM LEFT: Warm, rosy red walls, an old white and black stone floor, a Gothic bench with a long black cushion, and a handsome gilt-framed portrait all combine to make a cheerfully distinguished entrance hall.

OPPOSITE: In this corridor lined with thoroughly useful cupboards, the bits of wall that are left are hung with wallpaper, as are the walls in the bathroom beyond. White floors complete the feeling of fresh airiness in what, after all, is actually a windowless space.

Staircases

Altering the angle or placement of a staircase, or adding a turn, can totally change the perceived proportions of a hall. If replacing a whole staircase seems a bit much, you can still make an appreciable difference by replacing the banisters and stair rail, or just the stair rail. Again, it is worth reevaluating what you have and contemplating the difference changes can make.

A simple spiral staircase has been given an arresting orange-painted side wall, which works perfectly with the art on the walls. Note too, the tall sculptural spiral just behind that makes a visual pun.

Small, square recessed lights like these make excellent lights for stair treads. They are good looking, fairly inconspicuous, and give light just where it is needed.

Lighting

Lighting in halls, corridors, and on landings and stairs should be bright for safety purposes, easily dimmable for aesthetic purposes, and adjustable to illuminate any art or objects. Unless ceilings are particularly high, a mixture of recessed down-lights, wall washers, and the occasional angled spot for specific objects or areas, is a good solution. If there is room for a table, a table lamp is a friendly thing. All fixtures should work with a dimmer switch, not just because the softer light might be more desirable when safety is not at stake, but also because you can dim the lights down in a corridor, for example, for people who need to get up in the night, or for a child who is frightened of the dark.

If ceiling recesses are not adequate to allow recessed lights, there are various alternatives: track lighting, or the stretched wires that allow a variety of spots, down-lights, and wall washers to be angled from them (this last is particularly effective when ceilings are very high and recessed lights would be too high up to be effective). Judiciously placed wall lights could work well, though they do not do much for art. For a better solution, you could recess light strips behind a soffit or cornice built just below the ceiling all around the room to bathe the walls with light. If you are in a rental that you cannot alter, one with central ceiling lights and not much else, at least try to find interesting fixtures, like an old hall lantern or chandelier, or a handsome modern pendant, supplemented again by the odd table lamp (if there is room for a table) or by up-lights placed in corners.

Stairs must be clearly lit with the treads well illuminated. Those low, small square lights that can be recessed into walls beside the staircase are neat and efficacious. And do make sure that there is good light just outside the front door for inserting keys at night, to illuminate any steps or irregularities in a path, as well as for obvious security reasons. It is always a good idea in a house to have safety lights that snap on at the first sign of movement, alien or otherwise.

Flooring

On a visit to Britain in the sixteenth century, Erasmus was shocked by the floors in English halls, often called "marshes" and with good reason. He described them as "commonly of clay, strewed with rushes under which lie unmolested an ancient collection of beer, grease, fragments, bones, spittle, excrement of dogs and cats, and everything that is nasty."

We have at least gotten cleaner. It is now considered only sensible that whatever flooring you choose should be easy to clean and as tough as you can afford, since halls, corridors, lobbies, and staircases, even if they have shrunk to a fraction of their former size, still receive a good deal of traffic, not to mention the dust, dirt, and damp brought in from the outside. To obviate this latter nuisance, you should not only have a mat outside the front door, but you should, if practical, install a shallow well in the floor just inside of the front door that can also be filled with matting. Such a well will ensure that the mat stays in one place, will not fray, and will not be by-passed. Preferably, this should be done before installing a new floor, but it is still worth doing, if possible, on an existing floor.

The location of a home will make a difference to the type of floor you choose. Country, suburban, and vacation houses will generally benefit from as hard and tough a floor as possible, that is to say any surface like marble, terra-cotta, quarry tile, brick, slate, limestone, treated wood, vinyl, and linoleum. These floors can be easily swept and damp mopped from the vicissitudes of mud, sand, and snow and will stand up to pets' claws, children, sports equipment, and luggage and pieces of furniture being dragged in and out. Rugs can always be added for softness and color, but they should be secured underneath with grippe tape or with the sticky weave that is available in most rug stores and can be cut to fit.

Carpet is appropriate in city houses or apartments, as long as it is of a color and quality to be practical. Rugs can be laid on carpet and secured either with a sticky weave or, if they are not particularly valuable, gently tacked down. In terms of a hard floor for an urban dwelling, marble or limestone, whether in plain slabs or inlaid, always look splendid and have the advantage of visually enlarging any space.

If you already have a hard floor that you wish was different but cannot replace, there are cosmetic ways in which you can alter it quite satisfactorily. Wood floors can be stripped, sanded, re-stained (if wished), polished, and sealed. If the wood has already been treated several times and is now too old and too thin to be stripped and sanded again, you can apply an oil-based undercoat, coat it with an oil-based paint, and seal it with several layers of acrylic polyurethane (which dries much faster than the oil-based variety). Likewise, old marble, terra-cotta, ceramic, or vinyl tiles can be undercoated and painted over with oil-based paint, as can concrete, once it has been given a suitable first coat of concrete sealer to stop the rise of any moisture.

The delight in painting a floor is that you can achieve virtually whatever design or faux effect you want (such as marble or French parquetry), providing that the floor is really well-sealed afterwards with several coats of acrylic polyurethane, which makes it extremely durable. I have even, on occasion, stretched seamed fabric over an old floor, secured it tightly with tacks, and sealed it with polyurethane

Choose from:

- Marble, travertine, limestone, or sandstone
- Terra-cotta or ceramic
- Slate
- Stone flagstones
- Brick
- Wood boards or parquet
- Carpet
- Sisal or matting
- Vinyl or linoleum tiles
- Cork tiles

Painting a boring, old concrete floor is always a possibility. This one was painted to look like old limestone inlaid and edged with terra-cotta. Given several coats of sealer and polyurethane, it has lasted for years.

to make a new surface as hard as tiles. I have done the same, to quite dramatic effect, using a Greek key wallpaper border around the perimeters of an old wood floor that I first painted an all-over buttery cream.

If an old carpet is comparatively light in color, it can be dyed a darker shade to freshen it up and make it more practical. It can also be disguised by a layering of rugs, provided, as always, that they are well secured so that they will not rumple up, flip back, or be in any way a hazard.

Windows

Unless you have the luck to have long elegant windows or French doors leading off your hall, or an equally elegant window halfway up or at the top of your stairs, there seems little point in making equally elegant curtains. I think hall, corridor, and landing windows generally look better with shades, blinds, or shutters. Very small windows are often better just left alone; sometimes I put a couple of glass shelves across them, mounted on discreet brackets, to hold a collection of colored glass, porcelain, or an assemblage of plants. Other small windows look good framing a view if there is one, or you can add a plant, jug, or small piece of sculpture to cheer up the sill.

Furnishings

As far as furnishings are concerned, in addition to light fixtures, you will need a table or at least, if the hall is narrow, some sort of surface like a narrow console, shelf, or even just a windowsill for mail, notes, gloves, and all the other paraphernalia that inevitably collects in this

TOP LEFT: Two round windows on either side of the rear door in this hall are filled with stained glass. They look so good that the space has been left deliberately empty to ensure unalloyed enjoyment.

BOTTOM LEFT: A good, old-fashioned mirrored hall stand like this one is useful in many different ways. It can be used not just to store hats or coats, but also has a mirror for last

minute touch-ups to makeup and hair, and a surface for stashing mail and displaying flowers.

OPPOSITE: Ten precisely hung prints liven a white-painted corridor and staircase. The mirror above the Asian chest on the end wall effectively lengthens the vista, as does the long Oriental rug. Notice, too, the dark, polished wood floor that further defines the space.

clearinghouse for the home. Try to squeeze in a chair, or if there is no room for both a chair and table, see if you can find a narrow bench, which will do duty for both.

If there is no built-in closet for outdoor clothes already, try to find some sort of alcove (under the stairs maybe) where you can build one. Alternatively, if there is room you could install an armoire. If there is no room for any sort of closet storage, at least try to add a row of hooks and a hat and coat stand in an available corner.

Bonus furnishings, that is to say, anything other than necessities, are pieces that can be added if there is a reasonable amount of space. I have mentioned before that a hall (or large landing) is a good place for a desk and chair when there is room, and many house dwellers install home offices in the space under the stairs. Equally, I have seen compact computer desks and file cabinets concealed behind closets. Of course, in very large halls, especially

in older houses where there might be a fireplace as well, you could add a club fender, and install a sofa and/or club chairs to turn the space into an extra sitting room when necessary.

Accessories

Tables, shelves, windowsills, and other similar surfaces in halls and corridors can be dressed up with flowers, plants, sculpture, or other decorative objects. Walls in these link areas will take any number of prints, paintings, posters, plates, objects, collections, and general memorabilia. In addition to being useful for checking appearances, mirrors are equally useful for adding extra light, sparkle, and the appearance of more space. And, if there *is* the space, you can line spare walls with bookcases, maybe creating an alcove for a desk to make an extra study area.

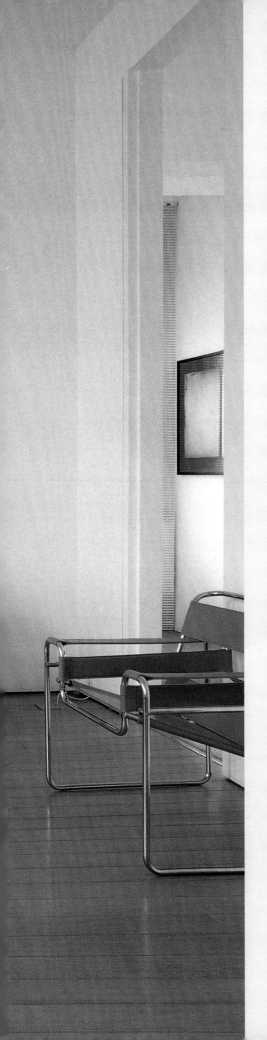

Living Rooms

LIVING ROOM IS ONE OF THOSE UMBRELLA TERMS
that conceal a multitude of functions. It is, of course, the
room in which you are supposed to do most of your general
living, but very often nowadays it serves as playroom, eating
room, entertaining room, and possibly a home office as well.

From Great Room to Family Room

THE LIVING ROOM IS THE AREA OF THE HOME in which you are supposed to do most of your general living and entertaining, as opposed to sleeping, washing, and cooking. Sometimes it is known as the "sitting room," while some people call it the "lounge"—both names descriptive of supposedly relaxing functions. In the old days it was first called the "solar," the first room to be built as an adjunct to the medieval great hall, where more or less every living activity occurred. By the Elizabethan times, most large houses had a "great chamber," which was used for eating and receiving guests, and oftentimes for sleeping. And even today some living rooms, if they are large enough, are called by the epithet of the "great room."

In eighteenth-century middle-class homes, the "living room" started to be referred to as the "parlor." Very often there were two such rooms, one at the front and one at the back of the home, with the front more formal and the back more everyday. More grandly, the room was elevated to a "drawing room" or "salon," in which case it became more of a room for entertaining and peaceful relaxation than for general living. When I was growing up, the "drawing room" or "living room" was the room that children were only occasionally allowed into by specific invitation.

The word "drawing room" is a shortened form of the eighteenth- and nineteenth-centuries' "withdrawing room," meaning literally a room one can withdraw to from the more masculine great chamber. From the nineteenth century, ladies mainly withdrew to this room after dinner, to be joined later by the gentlemen after their port and manly conversation in the dining room. Today, if anyone has the means and the size of house or apartment to have a drawing room, or formal living room, they more often than not use this room for formal entertaining, and have a family room or some form of general living or sitting room for day-to-day activities.

A living room or great room should really be big enough to fulfill both formal and informal functions. Nowadays, it very often serves as playroom, eating room, and possibly home office, this last only working well when children are absent. In studio apartments, a living room often covers sleeping and cooking as well. In fact, since it is so multi-functional, it could be called the "omni-room," although really, when you come to think of it, people with families and limited space might just as well call their living room the family room and be done with it.

Focus on Comfort

Whatever the nomenclature, a living room almost certainly has to be planned and decorated for a variety of different interests and age groups, unless you can encourage children to follow most of their interests in their own rooms or outside. Even so, it will be used, at the minimum, for listening to music, looking at television, reading, playing cards or games, and, but not least, conversation and the informal entertaining of close friends. Above all, it should be both a comfortable and comfortable-*looking* room, a room in which you really want to be. As a footnote, I would add that

BELOW: A good example of a well-appointed living/family room. A comfortable, deeply cushioned sofa positively invites relaxation. The floor to ceiling bookcase holds files as well as books, and the green of the walls are a happy combination with the rose of the upholstery.

OPPOSITE: A beautiful needlework carpet and delicate upholstery are kept pristine in this more formal, traditional drawing room with glowing, tawny tones, antique mirrors and consoles, Louis Quinze chairs, and matching table.

it should also smell good. Lavender and flowers in general, a whiff of wood smoke from the fireplace (if there is one), scented candles, the smell of newly mown grass, and just plain fresh air—all or any of these are a bonus to the senses. Ironically, since this is the room that generally involves the most thought and costs the most money to decorate, far too many living rooms—even if they are initially beautiful to look at—end up *feeling* rather stiff and stultifying because consciously, or perhaps unconsciously, they are designed to impress other people rather than to be personal, comforting, and relaxing. No amount of aesthetic pleasure, carefully chosen antiques, or cutting-edge design can make up for physical discomfort, or that slightly edgy unease that comes from the fear that you may spoil the pristine setting just by inhabiting the space. If the room works well for you and still ends up looking so good that it impresses other people, that is fine, but try to ensure that the room's "impressiveness" lies in the fact that it is as pleasurable and relaxing to *be* in as it is to look at.

To this end, surfaces like floors, woodwork, walls, upholstery, and tabletops should be practical and easy to clean, so that you are not constantly nervous about spoiling them. Keep the more exotic fabrics, carpets, rugs, and furniture for the more formal drawing room, if you should be lucky enough have one. But where there is only one living room, keep in mind that it is basically for family enjoyment and living and not to wow visitors.

The tranquility of this monotone room is highlighted by the dark chairs in the foreground, the lamp bases, the frames of the pair of mirrors on either side of the fireplace, and by the window shades. The seating, resting on its island of white carpet in the center of the pale floor, is quite obviously designed for relaxation.

Getting the Arrangement

The success and comfort of any living room depends to a great extent on the furniture arrangement. A good arrangement is one that allows a room to function well for everyday living needs, while encouraging the *whole* room to be used. In addition, a well thought-out arrangement should allow people to easily move around without disturbing others seated in the room. There should be at least a couple of comfortable chairs, preferably with their own footstools or ottomans. Good reading lights should accompany the chairs and an occasional table should be set beside them.

A furniture arrangement should also allow for a certain flexibility of seating. If, for example, you entertain regularly, you will need to expand on your day-to-day seating to accommodate additional groups. This means that if the room is large enough, you should have chairs, stools, and ottomans that are easily maneuverable. And although the everyday seating arrangement should be sympathetic to television viewers, this does not necessarily mean that chairs should be grouped around the television as if in a luxurious cinema. Leave that sort of arrangement for a media room, whose one purpose is to listen to music and watch a screen, unless, that is, there is absolutely no other focal point in the room, in which case the television can unabashedly become the focus. In this instance it needs to be somewhat aggrandized by having an outsized and/or splendid-looking set, or, more aesthetically, it should have a nice cabinet around it or be set in an interesting armoire.

Focal Points

A good focal point helps any sort of furniture arrangement. There is no doubt that the easiest focal point to arrange a room around is a fireplace—even if it does not work. Alternatively, there might be an interesting view to turn into the centerpiece of a good grouping. In any event, whatever the size of the room, try to make at least one good group of sofas and chairs to seat six to eight for conversation's sake.

The unabashed large-sized screen let down between the shelving units in this room turns the space into an efficient media room. Chairs with upholstered stools and deep couches provide comfortable seating. All of the lighting can be dimmed down as in a particularly luxurious small cinema.

An interesting modern fireplace looks something like an early Chinese altar with its fire-licked stones set on curved stell, all set amongst a bedding of wood chips. Such a fireplace would be a focal point in more ways than one, from its good looks, to its flickering light and ambient warmth.

43

Formal Rooms

IF YOU DO NOT HAVE THE CONSTRAINTS OF A YOUNG FAMILY, or have rooms enough to indulge the whim of a more formal entertaining room, then you do not have to focus on practicality. All the same, it helps, whatever the circumstances and the pocket, to choose fabrics that will clean well, and to make window treatments with generous hems that can be let down when necessary. However magnificent, original, and imaginative the decoration, furniture, objects, and art, I would still council that the upholstery and seating should be as comfortable as you can afford, the lighting as subtle, and the floor and paintwork as scuff-proof. I have seen too many interesting rooms spoilt by discomfort and fragile surfaces that have not been adequately maintained.

Here, too, if the room is to be used for frequent entertaining, you will need to allow for two or three groups of seating that will accommodate eight to twelve or even double that. This means that, as in general living rooms, you should have a mixture of seating with lighter occasional chairs, stools, and benches of various sizes that can be moved around larger, heavier anchor pieces like sofas and club or armchairs. The room will always look livelier if there are pieces of furniture, plants, and objects of different height and scale, and this applies to cabinetry and tables as much as to large and small sofas and chairs. Do not forget that you can always add to seating without taking up more visual space by installing comfortably padded window seats and adding a club fender to a fireplace.

BELOW: The good, flexible conversational group in this airy drawing room has movable slip-covered stools, as well as a pair of occasional chairs by the window to move around as needed. In this way, the grouping can accommodate any number from six to eight, or even ten.

OPPOSITE: Cushions on the large, comfortable-looking window seat in this living room follow the colors of the wide horizontal stripes around the walls, as does the large rug and even the lampshades. Notice the bulbs and lampshades fixed to the antlers hanging from the ceiling.

Small Rooms

Quite apart from the fact that a small room benefits enormously from a lot of mixed pattern, detail, and richness of color, you will find, surprisingly, that quite large pieces of furniture sometimes make the space seem larger rather than smaller. I am not talking about huge pieces of upholstery, but a judiciously chosen and placed tall armoire, a large painting or mirror, and an oversized plant can all add to the illusion of volume. Forget about most conventional seating however, unless you can get in a small sofa and armchairs. One good idea is to place a set of comfortable chairs around a fairly low table or chest to create a seating island.

In both large and small rooms, it is good to get as much variety in height as possible. A good deal of modern furniture is rather low, so try to vary the pace with taller pieces such as bookcases or an armoire. If you cannot afford tall elegant pieces, much the same effect can be obtained with a tall plant or floor lamp, shelves, mirrors, paintings, or a whole wall of prints.

This seating "island" surrounding and flanked by carved chests makes the most of accommodating several people in a comparatively small space.

Do not underestimate the difference plants can make to a room. Buy the fullest and best shapes you can and let them make a definitive statement. Put plants in corners lit from behind with up-lights; mass them on ledges or windowsills. The fresh green of well-kept foliage will brighten the dullest of rental furnishings and decorations.

Rented Accommodations

Many people are stuck at one time or another with a dreary rented accommodation that they cannot change because of the landlord's or building's regulations, or they could improve but understandably do not want to, as their improvements would only eventually be left as a present for future tenants. Anyone who, for one reason or another, has decided not to buy will have much the same problem. How can they make their rooms comfortable, efficient, easy to live in, interesting and fun, all for the least possible outlay?

If you are allowed to paint but do not get any allowance for it, try painting just the trim (baseboards, door, and window frames) with a contrast color—it will give an immediate lift to the room. If you are not allowed to leave nail marks on walls, hang pictures from the kind of extendible, spring-loaded rod that is available from most photographic stores. It should be slightly longer than the length of your wall; hang artwork from it with nylon wire or even ribbon. This same extendible rod can come in handy for changing your wall color at will. Simply run the rod through one or more rolls of seamless colored paper normally used for photographic backdrops, pull the paper down to the baseboard, and secure. (These rolls are available in some thirty colors in widths of 12 yards (9m), 9 feet (2.75m), or 4.50 feet (1.37m) and cost less than a single roll of most wallpaper.) Likewise, you can hang yards of cheesecloth from these extendible rods. Cut lengths to hang from just under the ceiling to the baseboard. Hem the cloth and thread through rods at the top and bottom, or you could just let the fabric hang loose. If you do this, loop the cheesecloth back over doors, windows and closets to allow space for opening, and fix it to the walls either side with thumbtacks or small nails. The fabric will hide a multitude of sins and can be taken down and put in the washing machine when it gets dirty.

It sounds elementary to suggest adding throw cushions wherever you can, perhaps a screen, a cheap table with a long skirted tablecloth, a throw over dingy upholstery . . . but well-chosen colors and fabrics can inject vitality where none existed before.

Decorative Options

Whether you are designing a new living room or redesigning your current one, it is expedient to realize that the space is not necessarily cast in stone (or brick, or plaster, or so forth). Sometimes, as I have mentioned before, there are reasonably easy structural, architectural, and cosmetic changes that can be made to a room without too much disruption and expense. And even if some do-able improvements are disruptive and expensive, they might well prove worth it in the long term for the difference in both aesthetics and the improved sense of space, scale, or proportion.

Walls

In the previous chapter I pointed out that it is quite possible to dismantle or cut through a partition wall between a narrow entryway and the room next door. Equally, if there happens to be another room, either at one end of the living room or at either side, and again if the wall is of the partition variety, you can open up the area either with an open archway or with an archway filled with double or folding doors. Or you can take the wall down altogether and define the difference in spaces, should you want to, with a pair of simple columns or columns and pilasters. Actually, even if the wall you want to change is load-bearing, you can still open it up as long as you install steel supports, or RSJ's as they are known in the trade. (This last option is expensive, and unless this is your own house you will, of course, have to get permission from your landlord to make such a radical structural change.) The room beyond can either be incorporated fully into the original room, or it can go on acting as a study or home office, dining room, children's playroom, or even kitchen. Either way, there will be a *feeling* of more space and if, for example, you give a party, the extra flow-through will be most useful.

If you do not possess any architectural details like cornices or various moldings, there is nothing to stop you

from adding your own (unless you live in the kind of modern building where superimposing architectural details would be extraneous). You can buy one of the many plaster copies of old cornices that are sold by the foot and have it added to your room under the ceiling, or, if you cannot afford this luxury, buy one of the cheaper fiberglass varieties. Alternatively, you can go for a stylish compromise with a paper border that will contrast with the paint or wallpaper, or use strips of burlap or grosgrain ribbon. These sorts of borders will also look good pasted over base or skirting boards or all around doors and windows, or used in place of a chair rail with contrast paint or paper underneath.

WALL TREATMENTS

When the room is mostly a family room and there are children and pets to accommodate, walls need to be tough and easy to clean. This presupposes paint with a sheen, or wipe-able vinyl paper and easy to clean woodwork and trim. You can liven up somewhat bland or characterless rooms by keeping walls pale but painting trim—baseboards, window frames, and door frames—a contrasting color. You can disguise eyesores—pipes, wires, off-center doors, and unsightly radiators—by painting the room a dark, rich color. This makes everything melt away into the background.

Deep, dark colors, particularly shiny ones or even lacquer, will make a room look larger than it is because boundaries and angles become diffuse and lost in shadow. They also work well with both traditional and minimal decoration, a cluttered look or a spare one. Somehow, darker rooms generally look better-dressed than pale rooms and certainly keep cleaner. And contrary to perceived wisdom, painting a dark room white or a light color does not necessarily make it look lighter and sometimes it will even look duller.

Equally, you can "panel" walls out in various ways. A good decorative painter can do it with paint, which always looks good. Or you can use strips of molding or picture framing above a dado, also framed with lengths of somewhat heavier molding. You can make rectangles or squares, or a mixture. Experiment sketching shapes to scale on graph paper, then draw them out on the walls with a soft pencil.

OPPOSITE: Here, a living room opens out into the dining hall beyond a pair of double doors. The two spaces can thus be joined together or closed off from each other at will.

Doors

First of all, you should ponder the position of your door or doors. It may be that moving one or all, or even getting rid of one, could make an unexpected difference both to the general feeling of spaciousness and to the wall itself. I have mentioned before about aligning doors in order to get a view into another area, and maybe even another still. Moving a door even a few inches on a wall could make a room look better-proportioned and provide added space for furniture and paintings. If a room is somewhat dark you might think of accessing light by changing a solid door for internal French doors.

A good many city houses from the nineteenth and early twentieth century tend to have their two front and back parlors or sitting rooms knocked together to make one larger space, while often leaving the two doors. It is often much better to get rid of one of the doors altogether, and it is sometimes more gracious to make the door that stays into a double door.

If your doors are unexciting, antique doors in various shapes and sizes can be found in antique stores and in yards selling old architectural details, or you can have them made to order. Tall, lacquered single or double doors can make all the difference to a bland room. I have also seen tall, folding doors made into a very zippy feature by simply painting each panel a different color or tone.

There are various cosmetic changes you can make to improve unattractive doors. They might look better stripped, especially if they are old pine, and given new hardware. Plain, utility hardboard or hollow-core doors can look a whole lot better if they are given false panels with molding or beading. This door has been made to look considerably more distinguished with its covering of dark blue fabric edged with beading allied to an aquamarine door frame.

If you decide to use wallpaper, there are tricks to make a less expensive paper look more luxurious and last much longer. You can use a heavy lining paper to hide any defects in the wall. Hang it horizontally and carefully line it up edge to edge so that no bulges will show underneath the paper proper. In addition, you can paint over inexpensive paper after it is hung with a coat or two of either matte or semi-gloss polyurethane. Test the varnish out on a small piece of leftover paper to make that sure the colors don't run. The varnish will deepen or "yellow" the paper slightly, but this generally makes it look richer and more interesting. The varnished paper will last longer and can be gently sponged clean. Likewise, you can make expensive wallpaper go much further by buying just a few rolls and using it as panels edged with molding or as a slim paper border, or by applying it only below a chair rail.

Beautifully patterned wallpapers, as pictured above, can dramatically affect the overall mood of a decorating scheme. A variety of paint finishes, from sponging to decorative brushwork, can also be used to add color, texture, and pattern to walls. In the room shown at left, the waving grasses painted over and above the baseboards are a nice touch of fantasy in an old period room.

FIREPLACES

I have never yet lived in a house or apartment without a fireplace and never would if I could avoid it. It not only provides architectural interest, but also a certain sense of well-being along with physical warmth. And the mantelshelf offers an excellent display place for various objects. If you live in a freestanding house or a top floor apartment, it might be feasible to install a fireplace and chimney where none has existed before. It is certainly worth getting advice from a good contractor or fireplace specialist. If a previous owner dispensed with the fireplace, it might still be possible to reinstate it.

If you possess a fireplace but have a mantelpiece that is not the right proportion or appropriate to the room, there is an enormous choice of replacements ranging from very costly eighteenth-, nineteenth-, and early-twentieth-century antiques to good reproductions, to an increasing range of enticing modern shapes and freestanding versions. Materials, too, range from marble, slate, stone and wood to modern bronze, steel, and fireproof glass.

If the proportion is right for the room but the mantel is in poor condition, it can often be restored. Worn surfaces can be "marbleized" by a good decorative painter. Good wood can be stripped and stained or waxed, or it can be painted either in the traditional manner, or again "marbleized." In the 1920s, 30s, and 40s there was a fashion for mirrored mantels and there is no reason now why mirror panels cannot be applied if the shape of the mantel is suitable, along with the style of the room.

Ceilings

You can make a ceiling seem much higher by painting it a lighter color than the walls and keeping the floor a lighter tone as well. Lower a high ceiling by painting it a darker color. Another way to make a ceiling seem higher is to "shade" the walls. Start lighter by the ceiling, then gradually deepen the tone as you get down towards the baseboards.

RIGHT: The twin piles of colorful covered baskets on either side of this cast iron mantel look decorative even when there is no fire.

OPPOSITE: The fireplace in this spacious drawing room is beautifully proportioned for the height, length, and width of the space.

Lighting

Before you even start on any alterations, let alone decoration, you should plan your lighting. Work out ahead of time what kind of light you want and where. Should it be direct, indirect, concealed, background, very bright or very subtle? Even if you cannot rewire (and any room in any building that has not been rewired for fifteen years really should be), or at the minimum add new outlets, you can at least reposition many lights for the better and change fixtures.

To my mind, lighting is the most important element to get right in any room, particularly the living room with its many different functions, all of which need to be lit appropriately. It is also the quickest way to change atmosphere and mood, to exaggerate space and diminish faults, to bring out texture, pattern, and color, and to highlight special possessions and achieve special effects.

Yet when all too many people think of lighting, they mostly seem to think of the vehicles for light—the lamps and various light fixtures and fittings—rather than the flexible medium that can be produced by electricity; a medium that can be controlled by the flick of a switch or the turn of a dimmer, as well as the kind of bulb that is used. So many people buy fittings for their shape, color, or looks but neglect to find out what sort of light they give out. Really, they should ask to see how the light works in the dark, just as they take fabric from a lit-up store to see what it looks like in daylight. Even table lamps with their various decorative shapes and coloring can give out different sorts of light. Older lamps tend to cast a more or less gentle pool of light, its intensity varying with the variety, wattage, and color of the bulb, and whether there are three-way switches and dimmers or not. New table and floor lamps often cast much sharper pinpoints of light.

Personally, I like to think of lighting as similar to cooking, with all the various subtleties and flavors you can produce by adding more or less ingredients. All living rooms need a mixture of background or ambient light; local or task light for working or reading; and accent light for objects, plants, paintings, and sculpture. Sometimes local light can also accent, as in a table lamp casting light down onto a "tablescape," or arrangement of objects. And I would include firelight and candlelight in the accent category as well. Dimmer switches are essential for any sort of lighting scheme involving spot, down- or up-lights, wall washers, or halogen floor lamps. If you cannot get three-way switches on table lamps you should try to get them fitted with individual dimmers.

Background or ambient light, the light you use to move around by, can be provided by dimmable recessed down-lights and other ceiling lights (hopefully not by a single ceiling fitting), backed up by lamps and up-lights, or wall lights. Any of these lights should be switched from the door. In fact, if you are rewiring and you can possibly install a second, five amp circuit so that *all* light fittings can be switched from the door, it will save a great deal of the inconvenience of searching and switching lamps on and off.

Local or task light requires exact positioning. Once you have decided which chair or sofa will be designated for a reading space, you will need table or floor lamps to the side of the seating, which can be brightened or dimmed as required. It is best to avoid trailing wires, although I know it is not always possible to conceal them. If you *can* do so, it is useful to have outlets inset into floors near such designated reading areas, or at least have outlets in the wall near enough so that wires can be concealed under carpet or rugs as much as is feasible. If you write, play the piano, play cards, sew or embroider, or take part in any other tasks that also need bright light, you should provide an efficient desk light, floor lamp, or down-light in the appropriate area.

Accent lights, too, involve several questions. Do you want just the odd painting or grouping picked out, or will you have a whole wall of paintings, prints, and so on, that will need to be washed with light? This will determine the

use of spotlights, framing projectors (the most expensive but most superior form of spot which can be manipulated to exactly highlight a painting or object), or wall washers. Equally, perhaps you will want to highlight plants, or a piece of sculpture, or some sort of grouping of possessions on a shelf or some other surface. Down-lights or lamps will cast a pool of light on any arrangement of objects, or, in the case of a bookshelf or glass shelves, a recessed down-light and up-light would be effective. Plants look splendid lit from below or behind by up-lights on the floor. Likewise, sculpture can be lit from above or by an angled spot from the floor.

Cosmetic Lighting

If you cannot do anything about wiring or installing new outlets, you can be more flexible than you might think by adding up-lights to corners and behind plants, sofas, and other furnishings. Mini, freestanding angled spots can be placed on the floor or on mantles and bookshelves to light objects and paintings. Even the central ceiling point or outlet, if there is one, can be used for track lighting or suspended wire lighting, or a recessed down-light if the ceiling recess is adequate. Then, of course, there are always more lamps that can be added.

OPPOSITE: The blue opaline lamp with the pleated shade is placed on a plinth to provide good light over the shoulder for anyone reading on the decorative Egyptian-style Regency bench.

RIGHT: What a find to discover a pewter lamp base to cast light on a collection of silver and pewter objects, as well as a mammoth antique key to add a sense of harmony to the whole.

Flooring

Floors can make or break a living room for they give grounding or foundation to any area and they add to the decoration, comfort, and, not least, to the sense of richness or space. Basically, the first choice to make is very simple, since it is between hard and soft, although very often both are combined; it is choosing what kind of hard and what kind of soft that is difficult.

In some apartments, in deference to neighbors below, there is no choice but to carpet the floor, or at the very least to cover as much of the area as possible with layers of rugs. In other houses and apartments a good deal depends on the location, style of building, and climate, and then, as always, on budget and taste.

Obviously, an informal living room will need something as tough as possible; more formal rooms can afford a more luxurious fragility. Rooms in hot climates are always handsome with marble, limestone, or tiled floors. Colder climates and city houses and apartments are made comfortable with wall-to-wall carpet with maybe rugs, well-secured, on top. Country and beach houses are usually better with a mixture of hard tiled or wood floors and rugs. Rooms with disparate furniture and furnishings are often well-knitted together with sisal, coir, or sea grass matting, especially in rural areas, though such matting looks good in town buildings too. Neither wall-to-wall carpeting nor matting is practical in beach houses where sand will settle in the pile or in the crevices, but rugs are good in these spots as they can be easily shaken.

In formal living rooms, gleaming, beautifully polished wood floors are a delight, but then so is a cool expanse of marble, limestone, or terra-cotta tiles. The sensuous luxury of walking on a deep velvet piled carpet cannot be denied. Likewise, Oriental needlework rugs and carpets are richly beguiling.

RIGHT: Double red trim is inlaid around the room as a border for this parquet floor. Its rich gold color almost exactly matches the frames of the furniture.

OPPOSITE TOP: This gleaming, beautifully polished and maintained dark wood floor has the effect of making furniture and objects appear to have a special clarity and polish of their own. Note too, the arrangement of pictures and sculpture by the side of the long, elegant window, which is especially appealing.

OPPOSITE BOTTOM: Glossy white paint and polyurethane were the only ingredients used on this floor, but they make the spare furnishings look nicely sculptural.

Choose from:

- Wood boards or parquet
- Painted wood
- Marble, limestone, or travertine
- Tile
- Terrazzo
- Mosaic
- Stone
- Linoleum or vinyl
- Carpet
- Sisal, coir, sea grass or rush matting
- Rugs

Before you make any decisions on flooring, examine carefully what is already there. If the room is covered in not very nice carpet or some other floor covering, pry up a corner and see the state of the floor underneath. If it looks promising, peel back the old covering still further to make sure that it is not just a wood border. If it happens to be good wood or a good hard floor of some other substance, it would be well worth getting rid of the nondescript carpet and, if it needs it, refinishing the surface underneath.

When I was growing up, pattern on the floor was mainly to be eschewed. In any case, it was considered much easier to work with a plain floor, given the perennial worry about how best to mix patterns. But such austerity with ornamentation is purely a foible of the last seventy-five years or so. All through the centuries a considerable amount of pride has been invested in the floor of the main living area. The ancient Greeks and the Romans made stunning mosaic floors, some of which are still extant. Elaborately patterned, often tri-colored marble floors, like those in St. Mark's Basilica, Venice, exist from centuries back. Old terra-cotta tiles, often with two-colored inserts, are still to be found all over Southern Europe and South America. Enviable, too, are all the numerous old European woodblock parquet designs made from different, often exotic woods, which were often cut and inlaid like marble.

Old carpets, of course, were equally labors of love. Quite apart from the massive number of designs and colors for Oriental carpets and rugs, there were the splendid French Aubussons and *Savonneries,* the noble complications of early Axminsters, and the numerous nineteenth-century needlepoint carpets and rugs that are so sought after today.

There is a phenomenal choice of patterned carpets and borders to choose from, and many designs can be made to order. But for those of us who can only covet these designs and materials from an admiring distance, there is always the comfort of what marvels can be achieved underfoot in paint, including trompe l'oeil effects and stenciling. And it is more comforting still to realize that all through the centuries people have been painting faux marble, faux parquet, and even faux Oriental and needlepoint carpets and rugs.

To paint an undistinguished wood or tiled floor, first coat the surface with an oil-based primer. Once dry, paint the floor with an oil-based eggshell or semi-gloss and finish with several coats of polyurethane. You can strip and stain an old floor either a grayish white, buttery cream, or plain white, then, if desired, add a stenciled border and top with a couple coats of polyurethane. You can paint boards alternating colors, or just paint them all over in a solid; or strip, bleach, and scrub the boards for a look that is particularly appropriate to an old or vacation house. (In the old days such floors used to be scrubbed with herbs to make them sweet-smelling.)

There is no reason, either, why one should stick to one material in a hard floor. I have seen successful mixtures of wood boards with a tile border; marble with wood; wood with tumbled marble tessera; and wood with limestone. Equally, I have seen some interestingly patterned floors made from inlaid linoleum plus a good deal of imagination and patience.

Windows

Windows are like eyes: they are looked at as much as they are looked out of; they also provide light, ventilation, protection, and sometimes the focus of the room. Windows can also make an immense difference to a space. I had some clients who had a large room with smallish square windows placed rather high up which were not only out of scale for the room, but also did nothing for the rear facade

of the house. I suggested turning the windows into a pair of graceful French doors. It was not cheap but the end result transformed the space, the sense of proportion, and the received light, as well as added interest to the outside.

Changing windows and window shapes will always be costly and can only be effected if the shape suits the outside as well as the interior of the house. But if you can lengthen a window or make French doors—or even add an interestingly-shaped window like an *oeil de boeuf* (bull's-eye), rondelle, or diamond to a high blank wall—the change to the proportions, scale, and light in a room will generally justify the cost.

Sometimes too, there are ways to change the look and proportion of windows without actually changing the windows themselves. I have added deep frames to the sides and tops of square windows, deep enough to allow a window seat to be built-in a foot or so below the sills. This is particularly successful on walls with two or three windows. The recesses that are formed between the windows can be filled in to make useful shallow cupboards, the windows themselves appear much longer and more elegant, and there is the bonus of the extra seating.

Windows usually have to be covered in some way or another, for even when the proportions are beautiful, the view stupendous and the privacy assured, a window covering is still the most practical way of filtering light in the summer and preventing drafts in the winter. The sort of windows that need little or no treatment are narrow horizontal or vertical slits of glass, small ovals, circles or diamonds, and stained or etched glass that only show a glimpse, if that, of the outside and are usually not able to be opened anyway. In cases like this, glass shelves with a collection, decorative object, or plants on the sill are often far better than attempting any sort of curtain or shade.

When choosing window treatments by far the most salient point to consider is what will best suit the proportions of the room and its style, and, as usual, your pocket. Clearly, enormously grand curtains with swags and tails and all the trimmings are going to look embarrassingly pretentious in a normal room with little or no architectural detail and none too high ceilings. Equally, plain Roman shades or blinds in a room rife with cornices, moldings, and a ten-foot-plus ceiling are going to look a little sad and bereft.

Grand-looking swagged curtains need beautiful fabrics and trims. You really cannot get away with cheap materials unless you choose yards of heavy plain cotton or linen embellished with stunning *passementerie* (the French

ABOVE: The pierced metal screen with a star design over this window looks interesting, casts intriguing shadows when the sun shines behind it, and would disguise a dreary view (if there to be one).

OPPOSITE: Oriental rugs and elaborately swagged curtains framing a bay window create a richly appealing setting. The crystal chandelier does nothing to detract from the scene.

umbrella word for tassels and fringes, gimps and braids, rosettes, and all the other decorative trimmings), which will almost certainly cost more than the fabric. Another thing to remember is that windows will always look taller and more graceful if you catch curtains back rather high, drawn up by strings or cords sewn invisibly into the lining.

Personally, I like curtains slightly puddling or dragging on the ground. And short windows do not necessarily mean short curtains, unless they are short cottage windows—even then, I prefer them long. If you do not want long curtains, or if there is not much room for curtains to draw back, you can use shades or blinds of some description.

Another attractive effect is to have full dress curtains with Roman or roller shades installed behind them, or just mount a beautifully trimmed shade. Another advantage of this sort of treatment is that you can experiment with different fabrics and trims.

Quite apart from all the different styles of curtains and shades or blinds, there are the varying types of shutters to be had, which look neat and uncluttered and seem to especially suit the current feeling for clean-cut, simplified eclecticism.

Furnishings

Many people seem to think that it is incumbent upon them to choose all the furniture that they will need in a living room from the very beginning and feel incompetent if they cannot make up their minds right away; but any truly individual room has to evolve slowly and this is half the fun and half the charm. In any event, not many people are able to start with a completely empty room. Almost everyone possesses either furniture from a previous home or room, hand-me-downs, or family heirlooms, and if you are one of them you will need to decide what you want to keep (and what to reupholster, re-cover, refinish, or repaint) before you start in on the wish list of new things.

If you *do* have to start from scratch, make a list of all the pieces that you think are absolutely essential together with a note of what they are likely to cost. If you get into the habit of perpetually window-shopping and checking the prices of furniture you like in stores, showrooms, catalogs, auction houses, and antique shops you will soon have a pretty clear idea of most values, whether of modern, antique, reproduction, or second-hand pieces.

I would say that at the very least most everyone would need the following: a sofa; two club chairs; two occasional chairs; a dining table and chairs (if you are using the room for eating); a coffee or cocktail table; lamp or side tables; storage of some sort; and lamps. The upholstered pieces should be as comfortable as you can afford.

Make a second "wish" list of other pieces you would like as and when you can afford them. This will be a more flexible list, as not only do tastes and requirements tend to change, but when you actually start to live in a room you often see gaps that you did not notice before, or realize that you have different requirements from your original thoughts. As a designer, I always council people to keep their rooms open-ended: furniture, paintings and rugs can always be moved around, added to or subtracted from, or exchanged. Items on a wish list might include the following: a round library table; console or modern side tables; club fender; small occasional tables; bookshelves (antique or new); bureau, bureau/bookcase, or desk; highboy, lowboy, or modern equivalent; jardinière; chest or chest of drawers; decorative screen; bench; upholstered stools; chaise lounge or daybed; and art and objects. In addition, you might add some fantasy piece or other as anything that lifts the spirit in a living room, or is out of the ordinary, is a bonus. I have a nineteenth-century dog kennel that I treasure, but it can be any fanciful object or collection.

RIGHT: An old corner cupboard with its inside painted red provides just the right sort of display area for an eclectic collection of porcelain and glass.

OPPOSITE: A Gothic chair, a charming writing table, a tall floor lamp, a screen, and a comfortable arm chair make an extremely pleasant corner in this calm drawing room.

Accessories

There are, of course, myriad ways to decorate a living room that are relevant to its use, shape, light, location, and style. If you have any hope at all of keeping a family living room tidy, let alone spare and minimal, there has to be a generous amount of storage which, if built-in, becomes more or less part of the walls. You can also get away with freestanding storage with the help of an armoire, cupboards under bookshelves, and small chests of drawers doing duty as side tables. Or, you can use screens and long tablecloths to conceal clutter. Talking of the latter, I am reminded of a small apartment in Manhattan where the living room, which was more or less a child's playroom by day, became quite elegant at night by dint of sweeping all the child's playthings under a large table with its equally generous cloth. It only took a minute and—presto.

There remains the question of how best to choose the color scheme. Sometimes this is dictated by possessions—a dominant painting, rug or carpet, curtains, and upholstery. Sometimes surroundings, climate, or location will help you with the choice between warm or cool colors, among other things. Likewise, you may have just always wanted a particular color of room: red for example, or green, blue and white, or white and cream. And sometimes, in a period house, the coloring of that particular era can be invoked.

The brilliantly colored painting (reflected in the wall of mirror) definitely dictated the color scheme as well as the design of the rug in this modernist space.

Kitchens and Dining Rooms

KITCHENS AND DINING ROOMS SHARE THE COMMON denominator of food, from its preparation to its eating, and indeed are often combined naturally in one space. Where they differ is that today's dining room furnishings are more determined by *where you eat*, while kitchens are determined by how you cook.

Kitchens

KITCHEN DESIGN IS SO MUCH WORRIED OVER TODAY that it is hard to imagine the fact that until the 1920s, most even mildly well-to-do families possessed kitchens that they hardly ever thought of, let alone visited. For the rest, as that great architectural historian Mario Praz wrote in his classic *An Illustrated History of Interior Decoration* (1964): "The kitchens and little dining rooms of humble people have always been, even down to our own day, the most conservative among rooms. In them, the functional always prevails over the ornamental, and frequently one may even say that decoration does not exist at all."

Over the last eighty years or so, the role of the kitchen has changed several times. New forms of energy, the development of labor-saving devices and appliances, and canned and frozen foods meant that by the middle of the last century manufacturers and designers had exploited the female desire to get out of the kitchen and turned the room into an aseptic, clinical, streamlined box.

Then came the cooking revolution of the 1970s and 80s with its new, newer, and newest cookbooks and television programs appearing as seasonally as vegetables. It restored a great many kitchens to being family rooms, if not *the* family room. People tried hard to make them warm, friendly, relaxed, comfortable, and above all, since the family cook or cooks insisted, workable and efficient.

This is the still life of crockery and food that painters of such subjects would die for, right down to the garlic in a small wooden trug, the basket of vegetables, and a special collection of covered cheese plates on the hutch in the background.

Kitchen Planning

If you have the luck to be able to plan a kitchen from scratch, it goes without saying that you need to make it maximally comfortable and easy to work in. If you are planning on a separate dining room, the two rooms should be as near as possible, bearing in mind the transportation of dishes and so on. If you are a keen cook and have a garden, you might also want to have easy access to any herbs or vegetables you are able to grow, quite apart from a terrace for outdoor eating.

Once you have settled on the room, you will need to make sure that you have ample electric outlets for appliances. Even if you cannot afford all the appliances that you would like right now, you should at least allow for their installation later. This is also one of the few rooms where ceiling light is important, so allow for that, as well as for light over the counters and sink. If you are planning to eat in the kitchen, make sure you can have dimmer switches too.

The sort of kitchen you want will depend very much on what sort of cook you are. A dedicated cook with a demanding job will almost certainly need extra food storage and extra-quick cooking facilities—as in a large freezer, pantry, and efficient microwave. If you have a family and spend a good deal of time in the kitchen you will probably want to make it much more of a family room where people can sit around and talk, and young children can do homework. You might include a stereo system or radio, and possibly a television, as well as a generous table for eating and an island or bar to sit at for a quick snack. If there is room for a sofa or a couple of chairs and tables, so much the better.

A mixture of gaiety and efficiency is not so hard to achieve and rewarding when done. Rose upholstered steel–framed chairs are set around a glass table on an expanse of pale, polished floor in this loft-like space, with a well-equipped galley kitchen behind. The whole setting is softened by the giant palm and the suspended paper shade.

BELOW: The ever-ready Aga is tucked away in an old fireplace in this functional kitchen that features an enormous refrigerator and deep freeze. The butcher's block cart in the center of the room is a useful, maneuverable work counter.

OPPOSITE: This all-scarlet dining room opens right out onto a white and scarlet kitchen as crisp and efficient as the dining room is cheerful. Note the blue and scarlet glass drops on the light fixture just above the table.

Apportioning Space

Kitchen planners usually suggest a work "triangle" based on the normal sequence of operations: preparation, cooking, and washing up. Since food preparation generally involves a good deal of doubling back and forth between refrigerator, sink, stove, and different work surfaces, the distance between these main work areas should be kept as short as possible. And each work area needs to have all the necessary equipment and utensils close at hand. The optimal measurements of this work triangle, we are told, should be between 4 and 7 feet (122cm and 213cm). If the triangle's perimeter is more than 22 feet (6.6m), you will be walking around much more than is necessary. If it is less than 13 feet (4m), there will not be enough room to maneuver comfortably.

Organize your storage around the various work areas according to what is needed: cooking knives, bowls, chopping boards, measuring cups, etc., near the preparation area; seasonings, spices, and herbs between the preparation and cooking areas; wooden spoons near the stove top; coffee, tea, and mugs or cups and saucers near the kettle and coffeemaker, and so on. As it may not be possible to get everything precisely where it is most wanted, think about the things you do most often and try to make the workflow for these tasks as streamlined as possible.

Measure the room's dimensions, allowing for the *exact* amount of space for doors, windows, structural columns, radiators and fixtures, and draw them out to scale. Make sure they are absolutely accurate; the slightest error can be disastrous when fitting in appliances and units. If you have an existing kitchen to work with, try to be flexible. It might be worth moving the stove, for example, as little as 3 feet (1m) from its present position in order to create a better workflow. Or to lessen the distance between the refrigerator and the sink, you might need to add an island unit to the center of the room.

Once you have traced out your basic floor plan and work triangle, you can develop the rest of the kitchen, depending upon the given space. Consider adding a workspace or an eating area, even if it is only a counter and some stools. If you cannot do everything at once, concentrate on your priorities or your worst problems, depending on whether you are planning a new kitchen or updating an existing one. When you have a firm idea of both what you want and when and how you can achieve everything, you can then work on finessing the various elements.

Basic Kitchen Shapes

There are six different basic kitchen shapes to work with, dictated by the shape of the room and its size.

THE U-SHAPED KITCHEN is generally thought of as the optimum shape for a kitchen, but it does depend upon having a good-sized rectangular room. The work triangle is easily accommodated; everything should be within easy reach with plenty of storage and counter/work top. It is useful to remember that a minimum of 5 feet (1.52m) and a maximum of 10 feet (3m) is necessary between facing base cabinets. One side of the U can form a natural dividing line between work and dining space, whether formal or informal.

THE L-SHAPED KITCHEN is convenient because by locating appliances and cabinets on adjacent walls you can create both a compact workspace and still have room for a decent-sized dining table. However, it works better in a large or long narrow room, rather than a smaller room where there is not the same scope for generous counter and storage space.

THE ONE-WALL KITCHEN works well in both a small space or in a kitchen/dining/family room where the emphasis is more on the general living theme than the kitchen. In fact the whole kitchen area could be screened off with sliding or folded louvered doors when not in use. Equally, it could be useful for a kitchen area off a living room, with the spaces divided by a counter or island unit. The only caveat

ABOVE: With the hi-tech dining table and wire chairs set up on a wooden platform beneath the mammoth square window, this all steel U-shaped island contains most everything needed in an efficient kitchen. Large storage cupboards are concealed within the pristine white walls, as indeed, they would need to be.

RIGHT: Crisp, stylish units all down one wall, topped with pale granite have an arresting dark backing between the countertop and long, open shelf on top. Equally long lengths of steel rod hold the *batterie de cuisine* (cooking supplies) near to hand.

LEFT: Here's a neat little galley kitchen that even manages to fit in a double sink and amusing display storage in the upper glass-fronted cupboards, as well as the regular things underneath.

BELOW: The space high above this narrow island unit is filled with a generously sized two-layered hanging pot rack. The sink with the cantilevered plate glass shelf is undoubtedly elegant and the red lacquered door provides a colorful counterpoint.

is that you do miss out on storage space, unless that is taken care of in various cupboards, armoires, or similar, in the living area.

THE CORRIDOR OR GALLEY KITCHEN can be as neat and effective as a well-organized ship's galley. Such a kitchen can save a good deal of wear and tear on the cook, but will not work for a family or dining area. Since space is usually tight, planning needs to be as ingenious as possible with slide-out and revolving shelves, and pull-out work surfaces and storage bins. There should be at least 4 feet (122cm) between the base units on either side if the space is not to feel crowded. If there is not enough space, it might be best to treat the area as a one-wall or L-shaped kitchen and build narrow shelves along the other long wall.

THE ISLAND KITCHEN provides focus and added efficiency to a large space. The island unit can offer extra storage and workspace, as well as perhaps a cook top (either self-venting or topped by an extractor hood), an extra refrigerator, sink, dishwasher, wine racks, and a breakfast/snack counter. If you don't have a cooktop and extractor hood, you can use the space above for a pot or basket rack, or simply have particularly good lights installed above to shine on the work surface below.

THE PENINSULA KITCHEN is much the same as an island kitchen except in this case a rectangular island is used to divide the working kitchen space from the family or dining area beyond. Again, this type of kitchen requires a large space to begin with but it is a neat way of adding an extra storage, or work area, breakfast bar, and buffet space.

Decorative Options

Beyond essentials, like refrigerators, ovens, and other appliances that enhance the utility of the kitchen area, furnishings, wall and window treatments, and decorative objects are the ingredients that give a room personality.

Walls

Once wall cabinets are up there is often not much wall left to cover in a kitchen. It is practical to tile the space between the work surface and the bottom of cabinets, as well as around the sink—unless the sink is right in front of a window. The tiles provide an easily wipeable backsplash. If you paint the rest of the walls, forbear to use a flat water-based variety because you will not be able to wash off the inevitable grease and smoke that accumulates. Instead, buy a semi-gloss or gloss paint.

Good colors with food are tobacco, cinnamon, sludgy green, and pine green. White, whether combined with blue, red, green, yellow, or pale camel or beige, will always look fresh. Either paint the walls white and color the woodwork or vice versa. If units are already a colored laminate as opposed to white or wood, choose a background that blends well with them.

If you would rather use wallpaper, choose a paper-backed vinyl, a vinyl-impregnated fabric paper, or paint regular wallpaper with a couple of coats of eggshell or semi-gloss polyurethane for a protective finish that can be cleaned easily. The varnish will yellow or mellow the paper a little but will also make it last a whole lot longer.

Other good kitchen wall finishes are tongue and groove wood paneling, or wide wooden planks, both of which should be waxed, varnished, or painted. Bricks, old or new, should be sealed with a masonry stabilizer or painted. And of course, walls can be completely tiled, which, although expensive, will need no maintenance except possibly in the grouting, and will be incredibly long lasting.

TOP LEFT: Vermillion painted walls with a pale terra-cotta tiled floor is definitely in the cheerful class, especially given the pink drawers and blue-gray painted cabinet and lampshade, which brings it into the Mexican color palette.

BOTTOM LEFT: This is storage as an art form, not as pure utility. In any event, the shelves make a helpful link between living and kitchen area, as does the dark wood floor used in both spaces.

OPPOSITE: Dark blue and white tiles are cool in contrast to the yellowish apricot paint and the collection of red jugs and plates on the top shelf above the work top, as well as the old earthen red tiled floors.

In kitchen-dining rooms you can make a division between the cooking and eating areas with a different wall treatment, or you can continue the line of the base units with a dado or "wainscot," or at least a piece of molding running at dado level with a different color underneath.

CEILINGS

If ceilings are quite high, it would certainly be worth lowering them, which will not only improve the proportions of the space but will enable you to more easily install recessed lighting, or add an acoustic-tiled or tongue and grooved finish, or an old pressed metal ceiling. All of these different finishes can be attached to the framework of the lowered ceiling. If you cannot lower them (say, in a rental), or if the construction makes it impossible to recess lighting, you can give the appearance of a lower ceiling by suspending track wires with spots some inches below the ceiling bed. They will look lower still if you paint the ceiling behind black or any dark color. If ceilings are normal height, paint them white to avoid complication, or any pale color to go with the rest of your scheme and to reflect maximum light.

Flooring

Kitchen floors need to be tough enough to withstand all sorts of spills, grease, and damp. They should also be comfortable enough to stand on for long periods and appear as good-looking as possible.

If you want a rustic-looking kitchen then flagstones, brick, quarry, and Mexican, Italian, or French terra-cotta tiles will fit the bill. Slate is splendid to look at in a slick, efficient room but comes at an equally splendid price.

Limestone or non-slip white ceramic tiles always look crisp and clean, as does terrazzo and the newly popular two-toned mosaic floors. Patterned non-slip ceramic tiles can be mixed in among terra-cotta for an ethnic look.

Well-treated and varnished hardwood floors look handsome and are comfortable and warm, especially in a kitchen-dining room. Linoleum or vinyl, or vinyl and cork mix tiles are generally affordable and are soft and light, making them ideal for upper floors in apartment buildings.

Choose from:

- Terra-cotta tiles
- Bricks
- Quarry tiles
- Slate
- Flagstone
- Non-slip ceramic tiles
- Terrazzo
- Mosaic
- Wood
- Linoleum
- Vinyl
- Limestone

Defining Spaces

If you want to make a delineation between a kitchen and dining area in a large room, use two types of flooring, say terra-cotta tiles and wood, or two contrasting shades or tones of the same color. Or you could simply put down rugs in the dining section.

The hexagonal terra-cotta tiles suit the brick walls in this warm-looking kitchen, made somewhat warmer by the vermilion-painted closet in the corner, the vertically hung prints, and the unusual—for a kitchen—full-length curtains.

Windows

Elaborate window coverings are definitely a mistake in any kitchen area, where they will pick up grease and smoke and in any case get in the way. It is far better to plan on simple roller blinds; cafe curtains (suspended from a rod set half way up the window by tabs); short curtains, or slatted blinds (if you are prepared to clean them regularly). Fabric should be easily washable. (If the window is near the stove or cook top, do not use any sort of curtain.)

Alternatives are glass or wood shelves stretched across the window to hold plants, pots of herbs, or glasses, or you can use hi-tech metal shelving. If you are really short of storage space you might think of building units right around the window. The window will then acquire a recessed effect and will need only the simplest of coverings or it can be simply left bare.

Lighting

Apart from the fact that you will need general light, work light and, if the kitchen is for eating, accent light as well, you should make sure that there is adequate light over every work area so that you never work in your own shadow. Therefore, I would say that the optimum lighting is to have down-lights and wall washers for the overall light; baffled light below cabinets for work light; and special lights over the stove top and sink. If you are going to use the room for eating make sure, as I pointed out earlier, that lights are on a dimmer switch and that you have either a light of some sort over the table, a plentiful supply of candles, or both.

Fluorescent tubes are best for under cabinet/work top lighting because they last longer, and there is now a good choice of different bulbs available to suit food preparation, like warm white de luxe or cool white de luxe, *de luxe* being the operative word. Mount tubes as close to the front of overhead cabinets as possible and shield them with a baffle or small cornice attached to the bottom of the cabinets to obviate any glare. Sinks will need a minimum of two 100 watt incandescent bulbs, two 75 watt reflector floodlights, or a halogen spot to focus light onto the bowl or bowls and draining board or boards. If you have an extractor hood over your stove top, make sure that the bulbs are enclosed to protect them from spattering grease. Island work areas can be lit by down-lights recessed into the ceiling or suspended on a track, or a fluorescent fixture containing at least two 30 or 40 watt tubes.

Old red polished tiles give what they used to call a "homey" look to the updated Victorian room. The table and chairs are placed on a rug to avoid too much clatter. The two long windows are left bare to allow for maximum light.

Accessories

Kitchen accessories can do wonders to help define the overall decorating scheme. Storage containers, including flour, sugar, salt, tea, and so on, come in assorted styles from sleekly modern to old-fashioned country. So do cookie and cereal jars, not to mention the variety of racks for herbs and spices. Drying-up cloths, bunches of dried herbs and flowers, strings of garlic and onions, and prints and wall hangings can all add to the general character.

Furnishings

Kitchens, depending on their size, may be furnished with dining tables and chairs, a chest or chests of drawers, bookshelves, an armoire or big cupboard, a desk and chair, and plenty of comfortable seats, such as rocking chairs, sofas, and armchairs.

If you are fortunate enough to possess a room with enough space to accommodate a generous-sized table (which can be used for both food preparation and eating, even if it's only occasional eating), it will inevitably become a gathering room, the sort of kitchen to which everyone migrates for a drink and a chat. Actually, if you don't have a table but happen to have a sort of kitchen/family room with a sit-up-to counter dividing kitchen and living space, you will find that the counter becomes the magnet. Even if the room is only just sufficient to squeeze in a small corner table or eating counter it will make the room correspondingly more friendly and the cook less isolated.

These friendly kitchen/eating spaces are comparatively easy to provide in older houses where there is already a large space given over to the kitchen, or where two rooms can be knocked into one. Likewise, the trend in new houses today is to provide just such omni or generalist rooms, in which case you might well get in a sofa, arm or club chairs, a rocking chair, music center, TV, as well as a desk and chair.

KITCHEN CABINETS

With pots, pans, dishes, utensils, and foodstuffs, among others, to store, cabinets are undoubtedly a kitchen's most fundamental furnishing, and due to the large amount of space they occupy, their looks can set the tone for the room's entire decorating scheme.

Kitchen cabinets and units can be bought in a large range of finishes, colors, measurements, and interior fittings, in prices ranging from fairly cheap to expensive. If you decide on a fully fitted kitchen, you will find that the units are made up of three elements: the carcass (basic cupboards and shelves); the doors and drawer fronts; and the work top (the surface which runs along the top of the base cabinets). Some ranges also supply matching "decor panels" to fit the fronts of built-in appliances (refrigerators, freezers, dishwashers, and so on). Many kitchen retailers supply their own designers who will visit your home to make sure you get the best results from such units.

TOP: All-white units with granite work tops and a stainless steel–fronted fridge appear clean and inviting, and absorb any amount of added color in the way of vegetables, herbs, and fruits.

ABOVE: Bright yellow, smooth-faced units, occasionally mixed with white, look sleek and cheerful, especially teamed with a white floor. Maximum storage helps the uncluttered look.

However, if you decide to work out an initial placement for yourself, it might be useful to know that heights for wall cabinets range from the very small 1 foot (30.5cm)—which is generally good for the space above a tall refrigerator—to 3 feet 3 inches (99cm). The depth from wall to front is a standard 1 foot (30.5cm), and widths range from 9 inches (23cm) to 2 feet (61cm) for single-door cabinets, and 3 feet 3 inches (99cm) to 4 feet (122cm) for double-door models. Corner cabinets with a single door and either fixed or revolving shelves can be mounted diagonally across a corner to use every inch of available space.

Base units mostly stand 3 feet (9cm) from the floor (if you count the work top, which is available in everything from various treated woods, to slates, marbles, granite, Corinthian tiles, and various vinyl laminates), in widths that match the wall-hung cabinets, in depths generally twice as deep (i.e., 2 feet/61cm). You can buy units with doors that open to shelves, and with drawers of different depths. Wide, deep drawers are excellent for pots, pans, bowls, and so on; narrower, shallow drawers are for cutlery and odds and ends; medium drawers are ideal for table linens. There are all kinds of refinements to choose from: glide-out vegetable storage; wine racks; slide-out chopping blocks; tall but narrow bottle drawers for oils, vinegars, and so on; felt or baize-lined silver storage; pot lid holders; tray storage; sliding trays for linens; and cutlery racks. Alternatively, you can buy standard but empty units and fill them with your own choice of "innards" or organizers. If your kitchen is big enough, you may decide on a central island unit. This may or may not house a sink or two and a separate cook and work top, with space for deep storage drawers, shelves, and a breakfast or meal bar.

Pantry or food storage cabinets are made to accommodate cans and dry goods like cereal, flour, rice, pasta, jams, jellies, and others. Often they are heavily hinged with one-can deep shelving from the top to the bottom of the doors for maximum use of space. Alternatively, quite narrow but tall storage cabinets can be made to pull out from the wall. They are available in full-length sizes or smaller.

Utility or broom cupboards (so often forgotten) are normally 1 foot (30.5cm) or 2 feet (61cm) deep (the latter best to accommodate vacuum cleaners and polishers), 7 feet (2.13m) tall, and from 1 foot 10 inches (56cmm) to 2 feet (61cm) wide. Similarly proportioned cabinets can be bought as housing units for specific models of wall ovens and refrigerators.

If most of these ready-made cabinets seem either too expensive or not to your taste, there are various other ways to go. You can buy unfinished or "whitewood" cabinets and fit them into your space as and where you want them, buying separate organizers for their insides if you wish, and finishing them off yourself with paint or stain. You can go to a custom cabinetmaker who will make units to fit the most awkward space in any material and finish you choose (expensive but worth it for a custom-built job). Or you can find a good and willing carpenter to do what you want, which might include cheering up unfinished units with a handsome wood or wood and marble (for pastry) work top, making shelves for cookbooks and odds and ends, and generally linking up old kitchen cupboards or armoires and chests of drawers with more streamlined units. For years every kitchen I possessed had either a large, old pine hutch or dresser with drawers and deep cupboards, or a massive Victorian "housekeeper's" cabinet, also with drawers, both of which housed an enormous amount of china and glass as well as cutlery, and they gave a comforting character to the space, as such mixtures tend to do.

Old Cabinets

If you cannot afford or are not allowed for one reason or another to do any major kitchen renovation it is cheering to discover that there are various comparatively inexpensive ways to cheer up the space and hopefully to make it work that much better. You can make a difference out of all proportion to the cost by simply giving your old cabinets a new coat of paint. A little more ambitiously, you can add molding to plain cabinet doors to give a paneled effect, painting the molding in a contrast color.

Drawers on the front of this hutch have been underpainted white and overpainted with two pairs of diamonds to ring the changes.

RENEWING WORK SURFACES

Tired-looking work surfaces can be recovered or replaced to provide an instantly different look.

- Plastic laminate surfaces can be renewed. Rounded-edge surfaces will have to be removed and replaced; square-edged surfaces can be re-covered with new laminate, using edging strips of the same material or by lipping the edge with wood beading.

- Butcher block is expensive, but it will turn your work surface into one long chopping block. Oil it frequently and sand it occasionally. Avoid using butcher block near the sink (where water will almost certainly warp its edges) or by the side of the stove top (unless you have

plenty of trivets available for hot pans and dishes) and it will look good for years. Let-in or rest on top a square or rectangle of marble or ceramic tiles for making or rolling pastry. Surround the area by the cook top and the sink with stainless steel, tiles, or plastic laminate.

- If you have woodworking tools, or better still a good handyman available to you, you can use planks of beech or hardwood butted together and edged with a rounded beading. Give the surface at least three coats of varnish, rubbing down lightly with wire wool between coats.

- If you are not heavy-handed with pots and pans you can re-cover work tops with tiles. Lay them on a chipboard or plywood or, if it is suitable, your existing work surface. Rub down the base surface with glass paper, stick the tiles with a tile adhesive, and grout in between with a synthetic plastic bathroom or kitchen sealant. An alternative is to add a special colored pigment to darken the grout. This will prevent it from getting too grubby looking. Edge the new surface with wooden beading, stained, painted, or varnished to suit the rest of the decorations.

- If you have rather a mixed bag of separate base units, you can make the room look more streamlined by installing a long run of work top to join the separate units. If the units come short of the length of the wall, you can create a tray or vegetable rack storage area by continuing the work top beyond the end of the units and butting it up against the end wall.

- Although marble is expensive and stains easily with wine, lemon juice, and other acidic liquids, it is useful to at least have a square of marble for pastry making. Granite looks terrific and is highly practical but expensive. An alternative to a whole marble or granite work top would be Corian. It is expensive but practically completely stain and burn proof and can be cut and glued like wood to create a virtually seamless surface.

Extra Workspace

If you have done away with all possible clutter and are still short on work-space, you can cover a sink with a portable chopping board, or turn a drawer into an extra work surface by fitting runners to a block of wood the same width as the drawer, so that it will glide in and out of the unit, resting on the top of the drawer when it is pulled out.

LEFT: At first glance, this looks like a nice little grouping of collectibles, but look closer and you will see how many small cooking necessities have been stashed away so that they are within easy reach of the preparation area. Sieves, cooking spoons, ladles, and so on, hang above the green platter and pot of variegated herbs. Wooden spoons and spatulas are set in the pottery jar, and a chopping board sits just under the windowsill, which is filled with storage jars.

OPPOSITE: Four iron bars of varying lengths hold pretty well the entire *batterie de cuisine* above this dark green Aga stove. Small wooden racks of herbs and spices are fixed to the stone wall. Note the two-toned units matching both Aga and chairs.

- A cheap and cheerful way to renovate a work top is to cover it with some sort of self-adhesive plastic. Smooth it tightly over the surface to avoid creasing, then give it a couple of coats of polyurethane. It won't be quite as tough as laminate but it will still wear tolerably well.

STORAGE

If you are planning a kitchen from scratch, be sure to plan generous storage for china, tableware, mixing bowls, saucepans (and don't forget shelves for cookbooks), as well as cooking staples—herbs, spices, condiments, sugar, flour, tea, and coffee—table linens, cleaning supplies, and all the other general kitchen necessities. If you are trying to improve an existing room, remember that the smaller the kitchen, the more efficient the storage must be.

If clutter is a problem, be ruthless and get rid of anything that you have not used for the last year. If an object does not deserve prime storage space, put it instead at the back or high up in a cabinet, or on top of a cabinet (a good place for casseroles).

If lack of workspace is the trouble, examine every square inch of the space for room to put extra shelves or drawers, as well as hanging bars or pot racks and hooks. Be sensible and re-think your organization if you need to. Try hanging saucepans from hooks hanging from a pot rack or pole suspended near the sink or stove. Instead of base cabinets have decks of deep drawers to hold all those large cooking items. Or, instead of drawers, simply have deep shelves with large wire or straw baskets. Spare bits of wall that are too small for conventional cabinets can be used for mounting pegboards for small implements and utensils; or pin-boards for recipes, bills, receipts, time tables, and reminders for yourself or your family.

Make better use of your cabinets, if they are not so fitted already, by installing swivel storage shelves. Awkward spaces between, say, the stove or sink and base cabinets can be used for racks for drying cloths or for storing trays.

Dining Rooms

DINING *ROOMS*, AS OPPOSED TO DINING AREAS IN OTHER ROOMS, are to be treasured. They had been somewhat out of favor for a great deal of the twentieth century with many architects, designers, and developers considering them to be space-wasters given the fact that one can eat quite comfortably wherever there happens to be room for a table and chairs. Now, dining rooms appear to be in favor once again as separate rooms, or at least combined with a library or even conservatory, to both of which they have a natural affinity. They need comparatively little furniture: a table, chairs, some sort of serving table or sideboard, perhaps a side or console table, good storage, a mirror or mirrors, and various candlesticks or candelabra. As long as you bear in mind that the room's main purpose is to provide a relaxed, comfortable area for food and its enjoyment, it can be as inventive or decorative, as theatrical or nostalgic, or as experimental as you care to make it.

The formal dining room, a room just for eating, seems so entrenched in the history of the house that it is hard to believe that it was actually an eighteenth-century idea. One of the first rooms formally called a dining room was designed by the great William Kent in 1732 for Sir Robert Walpole's house, Houghton Hall, in Norfolk, England. Before that, people ate, much as so many of us do today, anywhere that seemed convenient and could fit an adequately sized table and chairs. In the Middle Ages people sat at trestle tables in the great hall of the local landlord, and later the gentry sat in the solar, the first version of a sitting room. Sixteenth-century gentry ate in the great chamber or the saloon, or in small rooms off, while the rest of the population dined in their kitchens. Seventeenth-century people of any standing normally dined in the parlor, while the rest still kept to the kitchen.

Walls in these general parlors were commonly paneled with wood that was painted, grained, or marbled in dark colors. Alternatively, walls were hung with tapestries, or fabric was battened to the walls with nails covered with fillets of gilded leather or painted wood. Floors were covered with rush matting and occasionally with Oriental rugs. There was seldom a permanent dining table, most tables being brought forward from the side of the room and set up in the center when necessary. They did, however, have side tables consisting of tiered "cup-boards" (the origin, of course, of cupboard) or buffets, on which cups, drinking vessels, and plates were displayed and from which wine or ale and food were served. Nearby, there would also be a wine cooler made from copper, marble, or even—in grander homes—silver, in which wine or water could be kept at a steady temperature.

By the end of the seventeenth century, the smaller the company at dinner, the greater the honor, in direct contrast to previous decades where "the more, the merrier" philosophy held sway and large rooms were needed to house great groups of guests. Meals, as so often now, were set up on occasional tables, wherever people had a mind to eat: in the bedroom, saloon, or parlor. Cane-seated chairs were brought to the table from their places against the walls. These tables were generally oval or round with gate legs and folding leaves.

By the early eighteenth century the tiered cupboards had gone out of fashion and were replaced by the now ubiquitous side table or sideboard, which at that time was often topped with marble or stone. They were generally rather handsome and often surmounted by a mirror flanked by candle sconces.

Great Britain was really the first European country to eschew this flexibility and to design rooms especially for eating. Robert Adam, in his introduction to his plans for the remodeling of Syon House, just outside London (the equivalent to an architectural presentation today), explained that the English had to pay attention to such rooms because, "accustomed by habit, or induced by the nature of our climate, we indulge more largely in the enjoyment of the bottle." "The eating rooms," he went on, betraying the male chauvinism that afflicted

the British for centuries, "are considered as the apartments of conversation in which we [meaning men] are to pass the great part of our time—this renders it desirable to have them fitted with elegance and splendor, but in a style different from that of other apartments." Instead of being hung with damask, tapestry, and so on, he explained, "they are always finished with stucco and adorned with statues and paintings, that they may not retain the smell of victuals." He added that "soon after the dinner is finished, the ladies retire.... Left alone, they [the men] resume their seats, evidently more at ease, and the conversation takes a different turn, either gayer, or more licentious."

It seems that not only the conversation was less reserved. Louis Simond, a Frenchman normally living in New York and author of *Journal of a tour and residence in Great Britain during the years of 1810 and 1811* (Eastburn, Kirk and Co., 1815) was evidently shocked by the habit in certain gentlemanly circles of keeping a chamber pot in a corner of the dining room, which was apparently used quite unconcernedly, as needed, with no breaks in the conversation. Slightly, but only slightly more discreetly, the great British furniture designer, Sheraton, when explaining pieces of his furniture in his pattern books, much used by the Americans, described how the left-hand drawer of a sideboard was sometimes made very short to make room for a chamber pot cupboard below.

This stuccoed pilastered room with its paneling and statues, elegant fireplace and over mantel mirror, and splendid chandelier shining over all, could have been designed with Robert Adam's precepts in mind; the room is fitted with elegance, finished with stucco, and adorned with statues and paintings.

The traditional long refectory table did not become a permanent fixture in many dining rooms until the 1780s. Yet only seventy years or so later do we find Archdeacon Grantly in Anthony Trollope's *Barchester Towers* (Longmans, 1857) saying "There is something democratic and parvenu [sort of Johnny-come-lately] in a round table."

The fashion for reds and darker colors, used so often for modern dining rooms, libraries, and studies, began soon after 1800. George Smith, in his *Collection of designs for household furniture and interior decoration* (J. Taylor, 1808), says that "superfine cloth or cassimere [cashmere] will ever be the best for 'eating rooms' and libraries where a material of more substance is requisite than for rooms of lighter cast." He adds that crimson or scarlet are best, and that if calico is to be used it must be of one color in shades of maroon or scarlet. J. C. Loudon in his *The suburban gardener and villa companion* (1838), mentions that "few colors look better than a deep crimson paper in flock, the ceiling and cornice tinted to match." He also advocated a wood fire with large logs; a chimney surround of dove-colored, black, sand/black, and yellow marble; chairs covered in crimson leather with silk tufts; and an easy chair placed on each side of the fire. "In a closet," he added, "should be the utensils sometimes required by a gentleman after dinner. This closet should have thick walls and should be large enough for a person to stand in." At least this was an improvement on the barely disguised utensil so deplored by Monsieur Simond some thirty years earlier. It was also the start of the American powder room and the European cloakroom, which gave such rein to the decorative imagination from the mid-nineteenth century on.

Yellow and blue wallpaper trimmed with blue edging, blue and white checks, and white painted furniture give a light and airy feel to this room. Glass and tableware storage is skillfully concealed behind jib doors.

The Dining Room Redux

If you are in the position of actually having a room just for dining, there are, naturally, certain practical considerations to think about before designing a new room or re-vamping an old one. Ask yourself questions like:

- What is the maximum number of people you can accommodate for a sit-down dinner?
- How many people will eat in the room on a regular basis?
- Will the room be the only dining space, or will it be reserved for more formal lunches and dinners?
- Will it be used mainly at night, or does it need to look fresh for breakfast, cool for lunch, and intimate for dinner parties?
- How much storage space is necessary for china, glass, table linen, cutlery, and so on?
- Are your needs likely to change over the next few years? For example, will you have more or less family or do more or less entertaining?

Answers to all of these questions will almost certainly have a bearing on the kind of decoration you decide upon and definitely on the kind of furniture, size of table (or tables if the room is large enough), and the number of chairs.

Decorative Options

Dining rooms can run from traditional to modern, or anything in between. Most importantly, the dining room design should be in keeping with the decorating style used in the living room and/or other adjacent areas of the home. And bear in mind that the table setting becomes another decorative element in the room. Choose dinnerware and centerpieces that blend with the room's color scheme, furnishings, and overall style.

Walls

Since the nineteenth century reds and darker colors have been popular for more formal dining rooms, especially when candlelit. This is not to say that lighter colors will not work as well or sparkle as much, especially if a good deal of mirror, glass, and silver is used. Equally, there is nothing to stop one trying out unconventional schemes to make a striking setting. Wallpapers, murals, or borders can also be attractive. Whimsy or sweetness, on the other hand, are saved for the more casual kitchen-dining room.

Lighting

The same broad principles about lighting apply just as much in a dining room as a living room, whatever the eventual style of the space. You will need ambient light to get around and to eat by; good work light to set the table, carve, and serve at night; and accent light to show up special paintings, objects, and flower arrangements. In other words, lighting should be subtle throughout, but capable of creating different moods for different times of day (cheering on a gloomy winter morning; equally light, airy, and bright for lunch; soft and moody for a dinner à deux, or for what you hope will be a glamorous dinner party).

A mixture of recessed, dimmable down-lights, angled spots, and concealed up-lights on the floor, all backed up by candles would be the ideal. If recessed lights are out of the question you could, perhaps, try to conceal small spots on a track behind a beam; or use dimmable wall lights, up-lights, and a lamp on the carving table or sideboard, and any other side table. If you are going to use

RIGHT: Small shaded lamps housed in silver candlesticks cast a most agreeably gentle light onto this table. Note the whimsical frog plates and how they interact with the fruit and table greenery.

OPPOSITE: Various times of the day are well-catered to by the mainly concealed light and candle sconces in this charming octagonal room with its Gothic windows and doors. Note how the various design elements—the color scheme, furnishings, and accessories—are in harmony with the architecture of the room.

the room by day, on a daily basis, you should try to have as much concealed light as possible. There is something dispiriting about always seeing lightbulbs burning in the daylight hours. Up-lights concealed in corners and behind plants are good; lights concealed behind a pelmet to wash walls with light are another good idea, as are lights concealed in window recesses or behind shutters to give the illusion of sunlight filtering through. And a sculptural halogen floor lamp can give a big burst of light without looking too obvious. If you have any display cabinets or shelves, make sure that they are lit, and try to bring as much sparkle into the room as possible by bouncing light off crystal, mirrors, silver, and so on.

No one could deny that the combination of fire and candlelight is irresistible, but if you are entertaining and have older guests, you might need as many candles as possible, boosted by dimmable light fixtures—at least up-lights and perhaps dimmed table lamps, candlesticks, or candelabra. Incidentally, always avoid having the candle flame at eye height where it will dazzle uncomfortably.

If you have a hanging light fixture over the table, it should not hang less than 2 feet 10 inches to 3 feet (85cm to 90cm) from the top of the table. A dimmer switch and a rise-and-fall fitting will ensure that you get the correct amount of light and placement. An electrified chandelier, especially if it is made from crystal, should also be on a dimmer switch and will often benefit from a recessed ceiling down-light to light up the prisms. (Chandeliers, with candles or electrified, are almost as traditional in a dining room setting as an English mahogany table.)

Many people have decorative objects and paintings in their dining rooms that should be lit separately, unless there is a whole wall of paintings or prints that can be softly bathed with light by dimmable wall washers. Framing projectors will light a painting or piece of sculpture precisely without spilling light onto anything else, or you could use the best new picture lights. (Older, cheaper varieties tend to light just a very small part of the painting.)

ABOVE: Great attention has been paid to the table setting in the library cum dining room here: the tall and short vases of narcissi mixing with sparkling crystal and crisp white linen. The books and portrait make a dignified background. The entire room is bathed in light from a series of down-lights and wall-washers, creating an airy setting for a formal dinner or supper.

OPPOSITE: Up-lights hidden in corners, candles, and a dimmable spot concealed by the ceiling beam and trained on the nineteenth-century Russian painting are the only lights illuminating this dining room.

Flooring

Almost any floor will do in a dining room as long as it is not too clattery when chairs are pulled in and out; however, marble, limestone, mosaic, flagstones, slate, terra-cotta tiles of every description, are all beautiful in their own way and often dramatic, but are hardly quiet, so one might have to choose between general aestheticism and the occasional grating noise. Any dining room that is regularly used by children should definitely have a hard, easy-to-mop floor. Vinyl and linoleum are practical, relatively inexpensive, and quiet and can be inlaid quite dramatically.

If you really want a hushed quiet, then you need carpet. But do remember that corded, sculpted, and long pile carpets are inclined to harbor crumbs and bits of food; ideally, dining room carpets should be smooth enough to clean easily. Rugs on a wood or other hard floor can rumple up annoyingly or get ruined by too much chair movement, unless well-fixed with sticky webbing or grippe tape, available at carpet stores.

Windows

The way you treat dining room windows again depends on how and when you are going to use the room. If it is essentially a grown-up night room for formal dinner parties, then you can have quite sumptuous curtains to go with the often dramatic mise-en-scène of a special room for dining. If it is to be used in the day as well, then something more airy might be practical, or perhaps shades of one sort or another, or shutters, either louvered or solid paneled. These last can be painted to match walls, painted with a design, stained, or faux-finished in some way so that they, too, will look handsome when they are closed at night.

If the curtains are *really* sumptuous or dramatic, they could be subtly lit either by an angled recessed spot or spots, wall washers, a cool strip light behind a pelmet, or by floor-placed spots or up-lights.

Furnishings

I have mentioned traditional dining room furniture: the mahogany table and chairs, the sideboard and console tables, Georgian knife boxes and wine coolers. And, of course, there are all kinds of other lovely wood tables and chairs: the walnuts and fruitwoods, Regency lacquers,

OPPOSITE: Dramatically lined curtains, caught back to show their affinity to the tablecloth, stand up well to the barrel vaulted ceiling and the rather ecclesiastical paneling.

ABOVE: Traditional, but also certainly stylish, this room has both paneling and marble busts, chandelier and elaborate clock, wide old floor boards and classic chairs around the table.

and country elms, oaks, and pines. This is not at all to say, however, that nontraditional furniture is ill-advised. There are some beautifully designed contemporary tables, chairs, and storage to be found. The point about proper dining rooms though, are all the other interesting collectibles they will take, quite apart from the dressing of the table, which can be, and perhaps should be, at least for festive occasions, a drama in itself.

If you are buying a table and chairs, there are certain practical rules to follow, whatever the size of your room and the shape, style, and period of the chairs and table that you choose. You should remember that each place setting with an armless chair takes up about 2 feet 3 inches (66cm). Add 2 inches (5cm) to the width for a chair with arms (for example, 2 feet 5 inches/71cm). A long or refectory table should be at least 2 feet 6 inches (75cm) wide if both sides are to be used. Each person will

need at least 2 feet 6 inches (75cm) of space for getting in and out of their respective chairs. There also must be ample passageway around the table for serving and access, say about 3 feet 6 inches (100cm).

It is a good idea to try a chair at the table you have chosen, and spend some time sitting there to make sure that the seat is at a good, comfortable height and that it will stay supportive through long dining sessions. If you want to use squab cushions on chair seats, remember that this will change their height. Of course, if you have the chairs before the table, you should take one with you to try out with the table before making any purchase.

Incidentally, since antique, indeed, nearly all good tables are expensive, you might think of buying the chairs of your choice, but making a table out of block board and a firm support. Cover the table with a permanent floor-length cloth and add separate tops that will be easy to take off and launder.

These are not your regular dining room colors certainly, but the combination of rose, blue, red, and orange, combined with the dark wood floor is definitely upbeat. The exotic coloring of this striking contemporary room is matched by the rug and upholstery in the living area. The cutaway walls and large central vertical support, together with the wall of glass and generous square footage, lend themselves to a variety of interesting treatments. Small decorative accents, like fresh flowers and painted pitchers, can be used to carry along a color scheme.

Accessories

It is often pointed out that many of our memories of childhood homes are to do with dining rooms, most probably because so many gatherings of family and friends were held there. Likewise, many of our family heirlooms came from the dining room, not just now, but all down the generations: furniture of course, but also silver and glasses, wine coasters and decanters, tableware and linens, candlesticks and candelabra, mirrors and columns, sculpture and paintings. This more or less explains the generally traditional, often stage-set feel of so many such rooms, even in houses and apartments otherwise dedicated to modernity. It appears especially when there are other, more practical and down-to-earth eating places in the home that allow the dining room proper a certain license.

The late Mark Hampton, that most elegant of interior designers, pointed out in his book *Mark Hampton On Decorating* (Tandom, 1989) that, "searching for a way to blend modern stylishness with a fundamentally traditional look frequently leads to exciting and wonderfully original [dining] rooms." Which of course, it does. But one must not forget that in the dining room it is the table that is the real star—the table setting and the food—and everything else is really just stylish background.

Smaller rooms, especially rooms meant mostly for nighttime dining, benefit from rich, warm colors, achieved either with paint or fabric: Venetian reds, rosy reds, Chinese red lacquers, deep greens and blues, and Coca-Cola browns. One of the most striking dining rooms, which I must have first seen some thirty years ago, always stays in my mind because it had black velvet walls, a black carpet, black ebony table and chairs, black lacquer and gilt side tables, and gilt mirrors and candle sconces. The contrast was in the tablecloth, napkins, china, and flowers, which varied from spanking white and black and white, to brilliant yellow, scarlet, or emerald green. The lighting was concealed behind pelmets, inset into the ceiling, bounced up from up-lights on the floor, flickered from flames in the fireplace and the candles on the table, and shined from the chandelier above. It always looked quite stunning at night, but I cannot imagine it to have been much of a breakfast or lunch room.

Bigger dining rooms with several windows, or at least one large window, are easier to make pleasant for all times of the day. One striking room I had in London years ago had a shiny white floor, ochre-topaz fabric walls, a round black and terra-cotta marble table, black lacquered chairs, a large white and green marble fireplace (always with a fire), candle wall sconces, a lacquered Chinese altar table as a serving table, and painted white-paneled shutters. It looked airy by day, quite subtle and mysterious at night. In the winter, firelight and the smell of wood smoke played its seasonal part. In the summer, I always filled the room with plants and indoor jasmines. Which brings me to think of the charming conservatory-dining rooms I have visited, all sweet-scented and sun-stroked by day; even sweeter-scented but dramatically lit from under the plants at night.

OPPOSITE: Faux sandstone walls and a magnificent mirror with Gothic leanings provide a calm background for a fetching collection of gilded glasses and urn, old silver, as well as dramatically tall candelabra.

RIGHT TOP: Pink and blue bouquets of flowers, frivolous blue-edged glasses, and little blue glass bowls make the tabletop here a world of its own.

RIGHT BOTTOM: Cherubim and miniature box trees, rosy flowers, and sparkling crystal are all massed under the candles for this welcoming setting.

Libraries, Studies, and Home Offices

FOR MANY PEOPLE, THE LIBRARY, OR AT LEAST THE study, is their favorite room of all. For countless others, both rooms still remain an aspiration and first on their wish list when the possibility to own, decorate, and furnish one arises.

From Male Bastion to Family Room

THE LIBRARY HAS A FINE HISTORY AND ITS DECORATION, as that of the formal dining room, is almost invariably somewhat nostalgic. Even though there were few books commonly available up until the mid-1600s, Shakespeare can be quoted saying things like: "My library was Dukedom large enough"; or "Knowing I loved my books he furnish'd me from mine own library with volumes that I prize above my kingdom" (*The Tempest,* Act I).

In the seventeenth century the great increase in curiosity and learning fueled a similar increase in books, which were at that time mainly kept in gentlemen's (not ladies') closets by the bedroom and dressing room. In many cases, small rooms off bedrooms thus became studies furnished with a sturdy table often covered with green cloth—because green, then as today, was thought restful to the eyes—on which was placed a "reading desk" (at that time a small piece of furniture with a sloping top). In the latter half of the century, when books came out of the closet, so to speak, they were first kept on shelves protected by a curtain. A leather fringe was often nailed along the edges of the shelves to flick dust off the tops of books as they were taken down.

Samuel Pepys apparently had some of the first glass-fronted bookcases. There is a drawing belonging to Magdalene College, Cambridge, England, showing Pepys' library with five of these bookcases in an otherwise rather empty room except for a central round table with the obligatory cloth and reading desk. And he was said to have had twelve such bookcases made between 1666 and his death in 1703.

In the eighteenth century, bookcases were often integrated with the architecture, and it was at that time that the habit of concealing ordinary closets and jib doors behind rows of trompe l'oeil books with dreadful punning titles began. At Chatsworth House in England, the 6th Duke of Devonshire had titles inscribed like "Boyle on Steam" and "Barrow on the Commonweal" set amongst one of the finest collection of books in that period. The eighteenth century, in both America and Europe, was the great era of the library, when a good classical education taught the appreciation of the art of antiquity as much as the necessity for political freedom.

As the century drew on, however, and merged into the 1800s, this ostensibly male domain began to be invaded by women. That indefatigable chronicler and visitor to English country houses, Mrs. Libbe Powys, writing about Middleton Park, Oxfordshire, remarks that she found "A most excellent library out of the drawing room, seventy foot long—in this room, besides a good collection of books there is every kind of amusement, as billiards and other tables, and a few good pictures." Humphry Repton in his book *Fragments on the theory and practice of landscape gardening* (1826) shows a picture of a library leading onto a conservatory. The library is full of people amusing themselves in many different ways and Repton explains that "the most recent modern custom is to use the library as the general living room, and that sort of state room, formerly called the best parlor and of late years, the drawing room, is now generally found a melancholy apartment."

Sir John Soane, that splendidly innovative nineteenth century British architect, also describes his own library (and dining room) with evident pleasure. "The general effect of these rooms is admirable. They combine the characteristics of wealth and elegance, taste and comfort with those especial riches which belong to literature and art."

The Arrival of the Study

WITH THE OSTENSIBLY MALE DOMAIN BEING TAKEN OVER by the family, men were often forced into smaller versions of the grander libraries—the studies. A comprehensive picture of the eclectic late-nineteenth-century British study (and the very model, I think, of a study to be emulated) is given by Oscar Wilde (always a connoisseur of fine rooms) in his essay "Pen, Pencil and Poison" (*Intentions,* 1894). He describes the room belonging to his refined hero, Thomas Griffiths Wrainwright, as follows: "Wrainwright's study was a large room, its floor covered by a Brussels carpet with garlands of flowers. At one end was a desk with a silver inkwell on it and among the other furnishings were a Tomkisson piano, a Grecian couch and a table laid with a portfolio of prints. A Damascus saber hung on one wall and on another was hung a delicious melting love-painting by Fuseli. In one corner of the room there was a fine original cast of the Venus de Medici. Some hot house plants were lined up on a slab of white marble. On the shelves were books bound in old French Morocco of rare quality. There was an elegantly gilded French lamp with a crystal globe with gay flowers and butterflies and the chimney piece was balanced by a large mirror on the opposite wall. Illuminated by that lamp, the room was steeped in a Correggio-like light."

Today, most homes if they have a study at all, as opposed to the rather more prosaic home office, which is definitely *not* for anyone else to use, have a blend of

One mainly pistachio green desk and one bright pink one look great on the white floor. A row of recessed ceiling down-lights are supplemented by an adjustable desk lamp in this home office.

The tiny room shown here looks purposely built for an efficient home office, though the utilitarian look is considerably softened by the lively color scheme.

library-family room-study. The idea of the comforting clutter of the late eighteenth and nineteen centuries lives on with pedimented bookcases, bureau or secretary bookcases (or at any rate, good serviceable bookcases), light chintzes or bordered or trimmed plain fabrics, comfortable club chairs and sofas (sometimes in leather), skirted occasional tables, and the requisite globes and busts, desks or writing tables and desk chairs, paintings, prints, and perhaps a club fender if there is a fireplace.

All these, of course, may be mixed with better offerings and practicalities from our own period: good reading lights provided by well-placed and well-designed desk or table lamps, or angled brass wall lights, supplemented by recessed lights in the ceiling; comfortable upholstery, and often a sleep or convertible sofa for the occasional guest bed.

The Home Office

Even if there is no actual room for a library or study proper, there is usually space for a slip of a study or home office somewhere, where their owners can shut themselves off to work, write, and read. If there is not, there is bound to be space for a reasonably fitted home-office, or at least a bookish corner, with or without a desk, *somewhere* in the house or apartment. Landing spaces make excellent substitutes if the space is generous. If there is a window, you can build bookshelves around that and maybe even extend the windowsill in depth to make a desktop. Hallways are often large enough to be lined with shelves, with hopefully room for a desk and chair as well. Dining rooms are a natural, and most living rooms have space for shelves and a desk, as, of course, does the space under the stairs. In a one-room studio apartment, I have fitted a desk (made from two banks of filing cabinets and a top) plus shelves behind closet doors, with adequate space for a computer, printer, telephone, and fax machine.

Decorative Options

Certain elements, such as good lights, bookshelves, a desk or work table and desk chair, are fundamental to libraries, studies, and home offices alike. A run-down of useful ingredients for rooms from the grandest library to the most pedestrian, squeezed-in home office might run as follows.

Walls

Like dining rooms, the traditional library or study colors are rich and warm: dark green, deep grass green, or emerald green; dark cobalt, eggplant, or navy; deep apricot, terracotta, rusty red, Venetian red, lush rose red, burgundy,

claret, crimson, or Chinese lacquer red; and rich chestnut or Coca-Cola brown. These are all colors that go beautifully with books, wood (particularly that super library/study wood, mahogany), gilt, leather, and Oriental and kelim rugs. One word of warning regarding the reds: Although Venetian and Chinese reds look fine opaque, many other reds are much better and more lively topped off with a transparent glaze, or achieved by some sort of two-toned faux finish.

A less masculine, traditional room can be realized with gray or camel walls (achieved with either flannel or camel-colored wool or with paint), or with an all-over buff, or buff and white, perhaps with the insides of bookshelves painted

LEFT: A thick glass top on trestle bases makes a good looking desk, complete with a comfortable leather chair and an excellent light at one end of this living room.

OPPOSITE: Coca-Cola painted walls look distinguished in this handsome study with arched floor to ceiling windows, a creamy limestone floor, and red lacquered Chinese chair. Notice how interestingly this touch of red is reflected in the mirror frame. The tall, skinny desk lamps have deep brown shades that reflect light straight down onto the polished desk top.

red. In a hot climate, all white—white walls, woodwork, and floors, or a dry-scrubbed wood floor—relieved only by books, flowers, and art will look stunningly cool, as would a white room with faded gray woodwork and trim.

Lighting

Although our ancestors made do with rush lights and candles, and oil and gas lamps for their studying, reading, and writing (with goodness knows what strain to their eyes), what we lack in busts, statuary, rare porcelain, and rugs—oh, and space—we can make up for, at least to a certain extent, with lighting.

Of course, the first thing to provide is excellent desk/work light in the form of a desk lamp, preferably adjustable, or at least a table lamp that will shine right onto whatever work you happen to be doing. This should be as bright as possible with either a three-way switch or a dimmer attachment. Good reading light by chairs and sofas is another prerequisite. This can be in the form of a wall or bookshelf-mounted, adjustable brass, steel, or nickel wall lamp, hung sufficiently high to shine down on a book below, or an adjustable floor or table lamp that is again tall enough to shine down on a book. You can also mount recessed lights into the ceiling to shine down on a desk or worktop, or suspend angled spots from a track or wire. Again, these should be on dimmer switches.

Background light depends very much on the size of the room. If the space is fairly large you can use up-lights and table lamps, or up-lights, table lamps, and recessed lighting. These, too, should be dimmable. Any object or painting that you want particularly to illuminate can be lit from recessed or suspended spots, small angled spots on a mantelshelf, or, in the case of paintings, from picture lights. A whole wall of prints, watercolors, or photographs can be bathed with soft light from a suitably angled wallwasher, recessed or mounted at least 2 feet 6 inches (76cm) from the wall.

Flooring

I always equate Oriental, needlework, and kelim rugs with libraries and studies, and they would certainly add a certain amount of *ton,* or tone, to a home office. What lies under the rugs is a matter of situation and choice. In a cold climate, I would probably use carpet with rugs on top, suitably held down by a piece of not quite rug-size sticky webbing. If the room is not big, I might use carpet alone to make the space seem larger. Plain carpet can help to expand the visual space; a diagonally-striped carpet or one with a directional design will expand it even more.

Sisal, rush, coir, sea grass, or similar mattings always help unite disparate elements, deaden sound as effectively as carpet, and somehow help update a room (even though rush matting was used on floors centuries ago). They, too, will expand the evident space in a room. These floorings will look cooler, in both senses of the word, by themselves, and richer with the addition of rugs.

A wood floor layered with rugs always looks good, whether polished or "dry-scrubbed," especially if walls or woodwork and trim are in any way aged. If the wood is not in too great a condition, it can be stained or painted. Many old country houses, particularly in America, seem to suit a painted floor. If the climate is hot, stone or tiled floors are certainly cooler both to the foot and the eye. But again, I would probably top them with rugs, as much for the richness of color and pattern that they add, as for their sound-deadening qualities.

Choose from:

- Oriental or needlepoint rugs or kelims
- Carpet or carpet and rugs
- Sisal, rush, coir, or sea grass matting with or without rugs
- Wood floor and rugs
- Painted wood floor and rugs
- Stone or tiled floor and rugs

RIGHT: A faux leopard skin throw and kelims (not to mention the dogs) look comfortably at home with the books and polished mahogany in this traditional, formal library complete with a classical bust and gilded woodwork.

OPPOSITE: Long, straight curtains behind the elegant desk are a good foil for the desk's graceful cabriole legs and the extra-long corner cupboard.

Windows

As far as window coverings are concerned, much depends on the scale of the room, as well as the age of the books. If the room is somewhat small and the walls lined with bookshelves that surround the window or windows, you will only need a shade of some sort. A Roman or pull-up blind will give interest as well as protection; louvered or solid shutters will look neat. Louvered shades are appropriate in a more modern room.

If you possess old and rare books, you will need to protect them from the sunlight as much as possible. If you have the space for curtains, on brass or mahogany poles maybe, I would counsel using them in conjunction with louvered shades, blinds, or shutters to provide as much protection from strong light as is possible. In general, you can use much the same ideas as you would for a living or dining room, providing they suit both the proportions of the room and the style.

Furnishings

The minimum furnishings needed for a library, study, or home office would include a desk or writing table, a desk chair, and filing cabinets or cabinets of some sort for files and papers. Of all the bonus items listed, the use of which entirely depends on the limitations of space, budget, and style, the question of what bookshelves to build or buy, and in what form, are usually the most vexing, whether you are designing a whole room or you are only covering a wall in another room, hall, or landing space. Either way, the best thing is to build them in with the architecture, so to speak, in a way that will seem integral to the house or apartment. If you live in an older building with architectural details, and you are building floor to ceiling shelves, you will need to take special care of the cornice and baseboard detail.

If you are building useful storage cabinets below the shelves, the baseboards should be continued all around the room. Drawers or shelves can be fitted behind the cabinet doors to hold files, magazines, a stereo system, a small television and VCR or DVD (on a pull out turntable), a small fridge, and anything else you care to store. In one study I had the cabinets fitted with file cabinets on runners so that I could pull files out easily when sitting at my desk. Normally the height of such cabinets would be 28 to 31 inches (70.5cm to 78cm).

If you do not take the bookshelves to the ceiling, you should think of what you might want to put on top of the top shelf to fill the gap. Traditionally the space was filled with busts, urns, or Oriental porcelain, but you could add a kind of frieze of similarly-sized prints, etchings, drawings, paintings, or even photographs.

RIGHT: The elegant little writing table in a corner of this beautifully finished library looks everything that one dreams of in such a room. Note the floor lamp adjusted at just the right height to shine down on the table top.

OPPOSITE: The variegated stacking of these handsomely bound books is quite an art form in itself and makes a surprisingly distinguished design.

The bays, too, should be thought about with care and worked out with some sort of repetitive measurement in mind, like that of the door or window, or half the width of the door or window, if they are very wide, or whatever other proportion you care to use.

There is no doubt that a room completely lined with floor to ceiling bookcases filled with beautifully bound books is a splendid sight. With this patrician disregard for useful storage space, you simply treat the shelves as wall decoration and arrange your various bits of furniture in front of them. Another interesting arrangement, if the room is large enough to take it, is to build further bookcases at right angles to the existing wall ones, to create a private alcove or two. Whatever you choose to accomplish though, you must make sure that the bays (caused by the area of shelves between two supports) are not too wide so that the shelving will not bend or warp with the weight of the books. If you are custom-building anyway, you could also make cupboards among the shelves *above* cabinets, to conceal the drinks, television, etc., at a more handy level. These can be given paneled doors or some sort of grillwork.

There is, of course, a very large choice of ready-made bookcases and cabinets that are quite capable of being fitted together with moldings, and so on, to at least appear to be built-in. In a contemporary room, or workaday home office, you can choose from any number of good-looking shelving and storage systems. Or you could forget about built-in shelves and simply look for old bureau-bookcases, secretary-bookcases, mahogany breakfront bookcases, or free-standing bookcases varying from just under normal ceiling height to much lower. These last are particularly useful in halls, corridors, landings, or anywhere else where you would like to squeeze in a few more books.

Accessories

In addition to books, flowers, plants, sculpture, prints, paintings, and photographs are all appropriate accessories for libraries, studies, and home offices. The traditional globe or wall map; useful but good-looking calendars and desk accessories (like holders for pens and pencils, paper clips, and rubber bands), baskets or containers for correspondence and papers, paperweights, reading lamps, and so on, will all lend character to the room.

Apart from the leather chairs and rich warm colors that are traditional to such rooms, or the super-modern, super-efficient home offices, there is also the chance to fantasize around the serious work requirements. For very busy clients in New York who wanted their apartment to be based on a spacious Tunisian house, and therefore quite different from work premises, I got a decorative painter to create a kind of slightly dilapidated, striped Arab tent with a torn flap in the ceiling showing the 'sky' above. The desk had a faux copper top, as did the filing cabinets base, and the sofa, club chair, and ottoman were all covered in kelim fabric. The bookshelves were bought ready-made and fitted the available wall space exactly, and the floor was covered in coir matting piled with kelims. The computer, printer, and more filing cabinets were all concealed behind a looped-back curtain in striped cotton to match the painted tent.

Bonus furnishings:
- Club or arm chairs
- Sofa or Chesterfield (buttoned-leather or fabric-covered sofa)
- Library table
- Bureau-bookcase or secretary-bookcase
- Stool or upholstered bench
- Footstools or ottoman
- Occasional chair or chairs
- Side table or tables
- Coffee table
- Club fender (if there is a fireplace)
- Library steps (if shelves are tall)
- Paintings, prints, drawings, photographs, globe, decorative objects

Bedrooms and Bathrooms

THE BEDROOM IS THE MOST PERSONAL OF ROOMS, bar, perhaps, the bathroom. And just because they *are* personal and private, people should be able to indulge themselves in whatever scheme they like. I include bathrooms in this section because they are so often en suite with the bedroom, and thus often share some, or all, of the same decorative themes.

Bedrooms

THE ACTUAL WORD 'BEDROOM' did not become current until the mid-nineteenth century when it gradually displaced 'bedchamber' or 'sleeping chamber' or just 'chamber.' The 'chamber' word is not so very surprising when one realizes that right up to the eighteenth century, the bed was often incidental to this general receiving room. In fact, in the early Middle Ages and for several hundred years afterwards, the chamber was the exclusive province of the rich. Everyone else slept in the hall of the great house, or in outhouses or hovels. And in the early medieval days, right up to the fourteenth century, even the European rich slept on the floor, or on straw palliasses (thin mattresses) balanced on cords stretched across a low wooden framework. Furs were used for bed coverings and the only barrier to the outside cold and drafts were tapestry wall coverings and the smoking fire. I say European, for the ancient Eastern, Graeco-Roman, Middle Eastern, and Byzantine civilizations were immensely more sophisticated regarding creature comforts and luxury. Moreover, they had public baths or actual rooms for bathing, which were more or less unheard of in Europe quite soon after the Romans marched out, showing how quickly civilizations can decline. The Dark Ages were grubby ages too.

By the 1300s the primitive beds were becoming more usual. In as much an effort to gain privacy from the bevy of guests and servants who slept in the same room as to screen out the drafts and clamor, the bed began to be surrounded by long curtains suspended from a canopy attached to hooks in the ceiling. Alternatively, there were newer, sturdier, and more permanent

This richly canopied and upholstered bed is a good approximation of a medieval version, though I daresay a whole lot more comfortable. But the stone-walled bedroom with its beamed ceiling and sixteenth-century portraits, cannot look very different from a room of several hundred years ago, apart from the lighting, the upholstered headboard, and the apparent privacy.

beds starting to be made that had two posts at the foot and a solid headboard rising high enough to support a canopy. Real four-posters did not come into being until the mid-sixteenth century, and then had elaborate outer and rather lighter inner hangings. Since textiles were expensive right up to the eighteenth century, such beds and their hangings became major status symbols and were often transported around to various estates to avoid having to buy beds for different houses.

The elaborately carved frames and sumptuously embroidered wool hangings meant that for a time more skill and money was being expended on making beds than any other item of furniture. They were so big and the hangings so long, that they became virtually rooms within rooms. In effect, bed hangings were considerably more elaborate and complicated than window curtains, which did not arrive until many generations later, and when they did were much simpler affairs without pelmet or valance.

Given the importance of the bed then, it is not so surprising that people lay on their mattresses fully dressed to receive their guests. After all, the 'chamber' was still used as a form of family living room for informal supper parties, card games, and so on. However, when the bed was not in use as a daybed, the curtains surrounding it were kept closed, since the sight of the bedclothes could be construed as unseemly.

Matching fabric to the wallpaper is used here for the curtains falling from the elaborate couronne and caught up at the sides with bows. Notice the gentle trimming on the leading edges of the fabric. This mahogany sleigh bed is placed straight against the wall as behooved French and Italian young ladies in the eighteenth century. Bolsters at either end are balanced by tapestry cushions.

A Room of One's Own

The 1660s saw some progress for the bedroom proper. By this time, grand houses generally had one 'apartment' for a husband and another for his wife. An 'apartment' meant personal living quarters as opposed to reception areas, and ranged, depending upon financial circumstances, from a single bedchamber with closets off it to a whole string of rooms. By the eighteenth century in Europe, the bedchamber became a much more private affair, leading off the withdrawing room on the ground floor. The plan of large country houses of the time was analogous to a tunnel with the main reception rooms at the open end and the more private bedrooms, dressing rooms, and so on, at the other.

In spite of the general elaborations of this century, the bedroom started to become much simpler. Very often, the rather grand alcove that had been generally used to house the bed became more of a niche in the wall of a much smaller space. Elaborate tapestries and hangings gave way to plain wood paneling, often painted, and the heavy carved ceilings to lighter plaster traceries. But the biggest change was brought about by the import of cottons and linens from the Far East, which triggered the taste for simpler fabrics; in addition to these imported Indiennes, people began to use plain white linens, feather mattresses, and thin, washable, unlined cottons for window and bed curtains. This was in keeping with the introduction of new ideas for hygiene and less of a distaste for fresh air.

Nor were bedrooms any longer the exclusive preserve of the rich. The eighteenth century was the golden age for building, and various country, village, and townhouses were springing up everywhere. By the early nineteenth century, in addition to bedrooms

RIGHT: Boldly striped frames on a series of blue-matted prints immediately catch the eye in this bedroom. The thick stripes look good with the checked uphol-stered bed, the pile of lacquered chests and table, and the simple desk and chair.

OPPOSITE: The very simple four-poster frame in this tongue-and-groove lined room, has equally simple camel curtains at the head to go with the plaids on the bedcovers and carpet. The paneled dower chest is an appropriate size and scale.

being smaller and simpler, chairs and sofas were upholstered with removable slipcovers in checked, striped, or plain cotton; and painted paneling, bare brick, and polished or painted wide floorboards were kept deliberately unadorned save for the odd painting or piece of needlework, Oriental or needlework rug, or piece of Brussels carpet. Muslins and cottons were used for light curtains and bed coverings by both the upper and middle classes, together with the occasional new embroidered silk from China. As time wore on, printed copies of these embroidered silks on cotton became increasingly westernized and floral in motif, and eventually evolved into the chintzes we know today.

From the nineteenth century on, very little changed in the bedroom. Richer people retained their boudoirs and dressing rooms as part of the bedroom suite. In these suites,

Two glamorous four-poster beds, plenty of pillows, a dressing table cum writing table, generous storage, comfortable chairs, and a handsome screen, all the ingredients, in fact, one could wish for in a bed, or guest room.

the boudoir customarily contained a writing table, chaise lounge or daybed, and one or two comfortable club or armchairs. The well-appointed dressing room included a "sulks" bed, as it was often referred to, a washstand and dressing table, clothes press, cheval mirror, armchair, and perhaps a desk, one or two chests of drawers, and a large wardrobe. The bedroom itself offered just a bed and accessories like bedside tables, a couple of occasional chairs, and perhaps another chaise at the foot of the bed. Interestingly, few European bedrooms had pairs of bedside tables (or night tables) before 1760. Prior to that it was customary to have a chair beside the bed and the candlestick and holder was placed, rather precariously, upon the seat.

In fashionable nineteenth-century bedrooms, beds were often dressed in the same way as windows. Most curtains at the time were divided and looped back low, and draped gracefully upon the floor, rather than being of the pull-up or festoon variety so popular from the late seventeenth to the late eighteenth century. The alternative window style current during the first thirty years or so of the nineteenth century was to throw hemmed lengths of fabric over a brass or wooden pole with elaborate finials. This fabric was generally silk or fine wool with a contrast lining for effect. Underneath was a much lighter curtain of cotton or lace, which was supposed to perform much as the modern fly screen, keeping out insects when the window was open and filtering the sunlight.

In addition to the new Venetian blinds, roller shades were also common at the end of the nineteenth century. They were mostly made of "Holland," an off-white, red or green, occasionally striped, linen fabric, first made in Holland, hence the old-fashioned name of Holland blinds. And painted roller shades or blinds were also fashionable.

While arguments flew back and forth about the respective merits of various window coverings, wooden beds were giving way to painted cast iron and brass, and Cassell's *Household Guide* (1869–71) stated that "medical men consider it the more healthy plan to sleep on beds with as few draperies as possible." They suggested the half tester as a good compromise, with curtains that hung down from a canopy attached to the ceiling or wall, according to ceiling height, and projecting about half a yard (45cm) over the pillow area. In any case, beds started to take on a less formal air if their owners so desired, although the unabashed delight in a sumptuously luxurious bed with extravagant pillows and linens has never really waned and waxes more than ever today.

I give this abbreviated historical rundown on bedroom progress because very little of substance has changed over the last two hundred years or so, except for easier lighting, more thoughtful heating and storage, better mattresses, and easier laundering. All five have made a substantial difference to comfort, but basically, any ideas we have for bedrooms today are almost invariably taken from one aspect or another of the past. Ingredients might have been concertina'd a bit, but we seem to do well enough.

The ivory dressing set and frames, and the collection of boxes and fans all on a long lace mat, make a pleasant little still life on a dressing table set against white and blue lace-patterned curtains.

An old flag attached to the wall at the back of this canopied bed looks somewhat Napoleonic and military. This feeling is helped by the tasseled edged, light cotton canopy, the striped headboard, and the black-edged rug, as well as the somewhat battered pot cupboard used as a bedside table. Combined with the pale sky blue walls, the whole *mise en scène* is meant to give the illusion of being in some military tent on the field somewhere.

Guest Rooms

Guest rooms should not be personal. They will, after all, be used by a variety of people. But they should be welcoming to anyone, whatever their tastes, and they should be as comfortable as possible. There is no reason why they should not be a little theatrical, whimsical, or even a little over the top for that matter. After all, people are not going to live there. They have simply come to stay for a few days, so why not try to give them some special visual pleasure as well as corporal comfort.

Remember that the details count as well as the big picture. Begin with a comfortable mattress with a choice of pillows. Try to provide two firm, man-made fiber-filled pillows— *not* foam rubber—and two goose feather or down pillows, as well as two small pillows for each double bed. Use the best bed linen you can afford and provide good lighting, with candles and matches should you have a power failure. If you have the space, supply a good writing table and chair, and, if possible, at least one arm chair and upholstered stool, and a couple of occasional chairs. Do remember, too, to provide plenty of clothes hangers and a decent amount of storage, including somewhere for guests to put their suitcases.

Adapting to a Partner

Adapting single-bedroom accommodation to take a partner is very testing, whether male or female. I am not so much talking about the merits or demerits of masculine versus female decoration, though compromises will certainly have to be made, but rather of the difficulty in making room for one more person's personal effects. It can come as a great shock, once the all-embracing, all-forgiving honeymoon period is over, to wake up to somebody else's clothes and alien clutter all over what once seemed a well-appointed room. Although this is the stage when it would make sense to move or start from scratch, it is not often practical, so every possible inch of storage has to be utilized to cope with the changed circumstances and, if possible, to disguise the overflow of possessions.

Doors, and this includes the insides of closet and bathroom doors, are often an under-used ingredient of the room, ripe for conversion. Racks, hooks, and the kind of spring clips used for holding cleaning apparatus in housekeeping cupboards, can all be utilized to provide extra hanging space. Could you install a window seat? If you can, make it with a lift-up lid so that things can be stored inside. If you have not already got an old-fashioned ottoman, chest, or wicker basket for the end of the bed or under a window, get one. It will provide extra seating as well as more storage. If there is not room to add a dressing table plus a chest of drawers, think of buying three or four small, unfinished chests of drawers, the same height, and arrange them down one wall with a knee-hole or two between them. Paint or stain them to go with your room, then cover the lot with a long countertop of wood, marble, or whatever, and you suddenly have a desk, dressing table, and clothes storage all in one.

Stepped racks for color-coded shoes, neat piles of sweaters . . . it would be hard to find room for another's possessions in this carefully planned storage wall unless every possible inch of potential room in other areas was imaginatively utilized.

Decorative Options

Even more important than being visual appealing, a bedroom should be as relaxing and serene as possible. In addition to the bed, wall and window treatments, lighting, flooring, and even storage, work in unison to achieve the ultimate ideal of combined comfort and good looks.

Walls

Obviously the normal choices are paint finishes of one sort or another or wallpaper for bedroom walls, but fabric is particularly appropriate for its look of softness and luxury and for its sound and insulating property. There are a good many specially treated fabrics sold especially for the purpose, some paper-backed for easier hanging, and flame-proofed. The most common fabrics for walls are felt, suede fabric, wool, silk, moire, burlap or hessian, grasscloth, denim, firm cotton, and velvet. It is quite possible to put up almost any fabric, fixing it in position by one of the following methods:

STICKING: Firmly woven fabric, which will deter any adhesive from seeping through the weave, may be stuck to the walls like wallpaper. The adhesive must be applied to the wall, not the fabric, which should be pre-seamed for each wall segment, or the pieces carefully butted together over painted strips of the same color. This will disguise any splits. The more obvious seams can always be covered later with a fabric trim of some sort, or slim molding, as can the edges at the baseboard and just under the ceiling.

STAPLING: Use an electric staple gun and choose materials with the sort of design which will help to conceal seams. If you can line the walls with a layer of padding so much the better: the effect will be very like the soft, upholstered look of battening but achieved with far less trouble. Seam the fabric for each segment of wall before you start applying it. Any frayed edges can be covered with a matching, contrasting, or coordinated braid, or lengths of picture frame molding, or strips of brass, chrome, nickel, or wood beading.

A WALL-TRACK SYSTEM: This consists of lengths of track which you can fix all around the wall just below the ceiling and just above the baseboards. The seamed

RIGHT: The gently paneled walls are faux painted in this charming room. The heavy Indian cotton curtains are half lined and edged with a stunning embroidered fabric and the window seats are covered in a faded toning mini check.

OPPOSITE: The dark brown walls in this masculine bedroom make a good background for the collection of old sepia photographs, as well as a foil for the elaborate ceiling. The brown and white chintz bedcover and hangings meld in well, as does the honey-colored wood floor.

fabric is clipped into the track at the top and stretched down and inserted into the matching bottom track. This system is practical because the fabric can be unclipped for cleaning.

WALLING OR BATTENING: Upholstering a wall, or "walling" or "battening" as it is called, means stretching pre-seamed fabric over strips of battens or thin wood, which have been lined with strips of a synthetic fiber padding, often called "bump." This method is quite complicated and usually needs to be carried out by a professional, but the results are well worth the expense. It looks luxurious and its double layer helps to muffle sound and preserve heat.

HANGING FABRIC: Hung panels of fabric look especially soft and appealing when draped on the walls like curtains. This is a useful method when time or money or both are short, or to temporarily disguise the walls of a rental. Since the fabric is removable, it can be cleaned easily and taken away and used for something else when it is no longer needed for walls. There are several ways of hanging fabric: Very light and inexpensive fabrics like cheesecloth, muslin, or cotton sheeting, can be shirred onto stretch wire or long thin poles attached just below the ceiling and just above the baseboards. Heavier fabrics can be suspended from more substantial poles, either shirred, pleated, or from rings, and left hanging loose and just touching the floor, or just puddling onto it, but not so much as to trip people. I have also seen seamed panels of fabric attached to the top of the walls by a series of brass doorknobs, the fabric slightly scalloped in between. Catch fabric back over windows (use shades underneath) and doors, fireplaces and closets, and cover any bits of wall thus exposed with matching wallpaper or paint.

Lighting

Bedroom lighting should be as good to look at as it is to see by. It should also be restful and relaxing in general with punchier lighting for particular tasks, such as writing letters at a desk, making up at a dressing table, looking for clothes in a closet, and reading in bed or in a chair.

As always, you will need to think about the lighting plans for a new room, or an existing room you want to change, well before you start to decorate. Make sure that there are outlets positioned where the bed is to go, near the dressing table and writing table, if any, and near armchairs or a daybed. There should be outlets in corners for maximum flexibility (for up-lights, hair dryers, irons, vacuum cleaners, and fans).

If you decide on dimmable, adjustable swing-arm wall lights for your bedside lighting (and they certainly free up the bedside tables), feign sitting up in bed so

that you can decide exactly where on the wall they need to be wired in. You will want them set high enough to cast light down on any book you are reading, but not so high that they are a stretch to switch on or off. Incidentally, if you decide on lamps, make sure that they also are dimmable and are high enough and have the right shade to cast light *down*. It is a good idea to install dual operating controls at the same time you do any rewiring or outlet installation, so that you can switch on lamps and light fixtures by the door and switch them off at the bed. If you prefer reading in a chair or on a daybed, the best idea is to have either a table lamp on a small side table (again tall enough and with the right shade to cast light down onto your book), or a floor light of some sort.

If you have a dressing table it is important to have a fitting that will throw light onto your face. If you can have both top and side lights (as in those strips of small bulbs, often known as "Hollywood strips"), so much the better. Again, try to use them in conjunction with a dimmer switch, as they are so bright they will spoil the tranquility of any general lighting scheme if they are turned on full strength. Another solution is to try down-lights set in the ceiling above the dressing table and to the front of the mirror, in conjunction with side lamps. If you find Hollywood strips less than harmonious with the rest of your bedroom, think of having a pair of side lamps with wide slits in the shades so that you can reflect more light onto your face when necessary with a twist of the shade.

Light for dressing is generally provided by ambient light from recessed down-lights, or by a pendant light (or lights) with good shades for diffusion. If you prefer not to use ceiling light at all, you can use table lamps switched from the door, or wall-mounted up-lights, which will bounce light off the ceiling and give a soft overall glow. I always try to use pink bulbs in bedroom lights since they are so much softer and more flattering. Even better is to get lampshades lined with rose silk for *la vie en rose,* at least some of the time. Always make sure that you have good light in your closets and over any separate shoe racks, and that there is good light near a long mirror for clothing adjustments.

An almost monumental light fitting is suspended from the ceiling above this daybed and round table or stool. Luckily, the bay is spacious enough to take the overscale piece.

Flooring

On the whole, at least in cooler climates, bedroom floors should be soft so as to be easy on bare feet, quite apart from the noise and warmth factors. Rugs by the bed are all very well, but then you have to step off them on to the bare floor or coir matting or whatever, unless you have them scattered around like stepping stones, which is not such a bad idea if you can place them well. On the other hand, if a sense of aesthetics wins over the sense of comfort, or you live in a hot climate where looking cool is as much a prerogative as being cool, you might enjoy the contrast of a bare polished wood, marble, or limestone floor, or the coarse texture of matting, with a deeply sensuous bed floating like an extra comfortable island in the middle of the room.

If your choice is carpet, remember that the quality does not have to be as hard-wearing or expensive as carpet for a hall, staircase, corridor, or living room. Carpet for guest bedrooms can be even less hard-wearing.

Choose from:

- Carpet
- Wood floor with or without rugs
- Painted wood floor with or without rugs
- Sisal, coir, rush, or sea grass matting with or without rugs
- Limestone or marble (for hot climates)

ABOVE: Woven rush matting provides a good contrast texture to the beamed ceiling and heavily paneled double doors in this bedroom, as well as a uniting base for the eclectic choice of furnishings.

LEFT: Gaily patterned rugs are a fun contrast to the small red and white checks of the duvets in this long narrow bedroom.

Windows

The main aim in bedroom window treatments is to keep the room as comfortable and serene as possible. This precludes over-elaborate heavy curtains, but it does not preclude black-out linings, regular linings, and interlinings for those who cannot stand to wake up with the morning light. In any event, unless you want really floaty curtains that will lift gently in the breeze, good linings and interlinings make curtains look much more luxurious and hang so much better. Nor do they rule out having pretty curtains with all the trims your heart desires.

If you have the luck to have window seats, or just a radiator under the window, it would be best to have shades to pull down behind tied or looped back curtains suspended from rods, or a track behind some sort of pelmet, valance, or flick over curtain top. This will dress

Sweeping black velvet curtains are caught back by long tasseled cords set particularly high to show the white silk linings, as well as the white ceramic urns on plinths behind.

a window and make it look soft and graceful, without covering the heat source or concealing a window seat. If you do have a seat or seats, or have deep enough window embrasures to have them made, you should add plump, comfortable looking base cushions topped with scatter cushions. This way you can ring the changes with contrast colors, mixed patterns and trims, and at the same time make the room seem larger because of the sense of perspective given by the perceived depth of the windows.

Alternatively, you could have shutters behind curtains to keep out the light. If you prefer a more tailored bedroom, you could simply use shutters or shades of some sort on their own. Incidentally, if you do not like the early morning light and you decide on fabric shades, make sure they overlap the window's frame so that no chinks of light sneak through the sides. Also be sure to stress to whoever is making them that you want proper black-out backing. This narrows down the field to either custom-made Roman or roller shades, because it is pretty well impossible to laminate black-out material onto ready-made shades, and Austrian, festoon, and pull-up curtains only look good in light, rather filmy fabrics. Again, if the room is not all that large, you could have shutters or shades and leave the drama to an elaborate bed with hangings and all the rest.

If a window faces onto a street so that you need privacy, think of using some sort of louvered shade, or a shade that lets the light in without allowing a view of the room's interior. An alternative is to install a white roller shade that pulls up from the bottom, rather than down from the top, so that you can get the right degree of privacy without losing too much light.

SPECIAL EFFECTS

If your windows are less than perfect (or disproportionate to the room), it is quite easy to change their look and apparent proportion depending on the sort of window treatments you give them:

TO MAKE A SHORT WINDOW LOOK TALLER fix the curtain rod or track 6 to 8 inches (15–20cm) above the top of the frame (if, that is, you have the wall space). This is most effective at night when the curtains are drawn. However, if you fix a deep pelmet or valance about 8 inches (20cm) above the frame to hide the wall above the frame, the windows will look taller by day as well as by night.

Two sets of gracefully drawn back curtains plus a Roman shade fill this large window bay. The inner curtains could be released from their good-looking round hold-backs, but more often one would only need to let down the shade. Note the small gilt cherubim at the ends of the mahogany pole fixed under the plaster cornice.

TO MAKE A NARROW WINDOW LOOK WIDER choose a wider rod or track than the window frame so that the curtains hang on either side of the frame, obscuring it but not overlapping any part of the window. This will also let in the maximum amount of light.

TO MAKE A TALL WINDOW LOOK SHORTER (which is somewhat rare, but occasionally in old houses converted to apartments, especially when a large room has been divided, windows can be out of proportion to the size of the new space), put up a deep, shaped pelmet or gathered valance, which will distract the eye from the expanse of glass.

TO MAKE A WIDE WINDOW LOOK NARROWER design curtains that meet in the middle at the top of the window, and loop them back high at the sides with Russian stringing (strings or tapes sewn into the lining of the curtain so that they can be looped back gracefully without tie-backs or hold backs). Or just loop them back in any way you like.

TO MAKE A SMALL, HIGH, BUT WIDE WINDOW LOOK LARGER consider making a deep platform at sill height reached by shallow carpeted steps. This not only creates

a good lounging area (and with a mattress and sleeping bag on top, a good sleep-over space), but will also make the room look much more interesting. A less complicated solution is to use horizontal louvered shades.

TO MAKE THE MOST OF AN ARCHED FRAME try to fix a curved track, pelmet, or valance to follow the contours of the window and have the curtains meet at the top and loop back at the sides either by Russian stringing or tie or hold backs. If this is difficult for some reason, though curved or bendable tracks are now easily available, put up a track, rod, or pole high enough and wide enough to allow curtains to clear the frame by day (at night, alas, the arch will be lost).

Bed Hangings

If you have bed hangings as well as curtains, it is more restful, that is to say less jarring to treat them in much the same way; not necessarily in the same fashion, but certainly in the same fabrics and patterns, which can also be used for any upholstery in the room. This was an eighteenth-century habit, particularly in France and Britain, and still greatly practiced by the French, and it certainly provides a calming background.

Furnishings

As I have already mentioned, bedrooms are essentially personal rooms and there are really no particular rules to follow, except that I reiterate that they should be as comfortable as it is possible to make them. And I am not still talking about the bed. The room should be comfortable all over: comfortable lighting (at the right height and intensity); comfortable seating; comfortable, well-organized storage; nicely-lined drawers and cupboards complete with sweet-smelling sachets (renewed often); curtains and shades that pull easily and fit well. It is true that standards of comfort vary wildly. What is seductively opulent for one is suffocating for another who is more comfortable with simplicity and clarity of line.

Apart from a bed, a minimum of furnishings would include bedside tables (they need not be matching, but it helps if they are of the same height) and bedside lights, at least one chair, closets, and bureaus or chests of drawers. For bonus furnishings, you may choose: a writing table; dressing table and mirror (with suitable lighting); comfortable club or armchairs and upholstered stools with adjoining lamps; daybed with an adjoining light; chest or ottoman; bookcase; side tables; and a long and/or ornamental mirror.

BED TREATMENTS

Both Renaissance and cinquecento genre and even religious Italian paintings, as well as later European paintings right up to the nineteenth century, often contain the most marvelous inspirations for elaborate beds and

bed hangings, not just for the different shapes but also for their use of color contrasts, trims, and mixed patterns in the various fabrics. If you don't see such early bed treatments in paintings, you can certainly see wonderful late seventeenth- and eighteenth-century versions in period rooms in museums worldwide, as well as in grand houses open to the public both in America and Europe.

The heavily carved and turned British Tudor beds still extant, with their old velvet or crewel hangings; the complicated and luxurious hangings produced in the seventeenth century in Spain, France, the Netherlands, and Britain; the amazing late-seventeenth-century Baroque canopies, mainly suspended from the ceiling and pasted all over with damask or velvet; the lighter, frothier, often quite outrageous Rococo beds of eighteenth-century Europe; those graceful, supremely elegant *lits a la Polonaise* with their small rounded canopies supported by rods tapering in from wooden bedposts, all swagged and tasseled, corded and rosetted (the Getty Museum in Los Angeles has a marvelous example); all of these must have cost relatively as much then as an expensive car does today.

The "sweetness and light" of the Queen Anne Revival in the late nineteenth and early twentieth century, and the sudden craze for fresh air at all costs, made beds a great deal simpler, and any hangings, a good deal lighter. This,

followed by the determined lack of ornamentation and push for austerity in decoration (caused by modernism and the Bauhaus Movement), plus a certain reluctance on the part of the older American families not to put on any sort of show, put an end to the more profligate of the extravaganzas. Still, there were some pretty sumptuous beds produced in the 1920s and 30s, like variations on the upholstered sleigh beds, often with panels of silk or satin hung behind the bedhead from a pole, or scalloped and caught with fastenings of one kind or another. In all this, one should not, of course, forget the charming *noncurtained* four-posted colonial beds, emulated in a way today, by those spare and elegant steel or iron four-posters, meant to be kept bare.

Whatever style of bed or beds you choose, I do think you should pay as much attention to the mattresses, headboards, linens, pillows, duvets, blankets and bedspreads or quilts as you can, to ensure that they are of as good a quality as you can afford. If you come across old linens at all, do always try to buy them, there is nothing so seductive in or on a bed as old, pure linen sheets and bedcovers, or as pure-looking.

The comfort of a bed is as important—more important—than its looks, though to achieve both is the ideal. And there is no point in having a beautifully beguiling bed if the bedclothes are untidy, so the way you make a bed up is as fundamental to its looks as how you dress it.

VARIATIONS ON A THEME

Although many of the more seductive and sumptuous beds of the past are out of sight for most people, there are all kinds of variations that are not too outrageous to carry out. Try any of the following:

- Drape a length of fabric over a short rod suspended at right angles over the bedhead.
- Drape lengths of fabric gracefully from couronnes or a rondelle above a bed to make a kind of baldachin.
- Make "four-posters" from four lengths of fabric suspended from the ceiling, or from a 2 × 4 frame slightly bigger than the bed fixed to the ceiling. Adhere hook-and-loop fastener (Velcro) to the frame and fabric respectively, so the curtains can be taken down for cleaning. Make a pelmet or valance to disguise the frame and you get more or less instant elegance.

Accessories

Decorations and furnishings are inseparable in the case of bedrooms, in the sense that they should be as personal as possible, and, like all of the other decorative elements in the room, bedroom accessories should enhance the comfort and calm of the room. Embellish walls with paintings, prints, and objects. Place bowls of potpourri and/or aromatic candles, as well as family photographs, on tabletops. Have glasses and carafes of fresh water, or mineral water, and boxes of tissues always at hand. Wastepaper baskets should be capacious and good-looking. Adorn dressing tables and dressers with easy arrangements of personal collections, and always have plenty of books stacked on tables and readily available for a relaxing diversion.

LEFT TOP: This upholstered bedhead in this very personal room is topped by a gilded wooden swag, which looks peculiarly appropriate under the pleasing grouping of paintings, prints, and mirrors. Notice the Corinthian capital used as a side table and the glass wall lamps on either side of the bed.

LEFT BOTTOM: Swing-arm lamps are fixed at just the right height either side of the necklace-strung headboard to make it easy on the eyes. A collection of prints, photographs, paintings, carvings, and mirrors line the walls, and boxes and this and that cover pretty well every surface. There is no obvious attempt at decoration as such—the room is clearly arranged to suit the owner—but the general effect is nonetheless decorative.

OPPOSITE: This elegant modern iron four-poster is meant to be kept more or less bare, except for the requisite but elegant mosquito net. The bed is quite sculptural enough.

Storage

Bedroom storage has to take care of most, if not all of our personal possessions, so it must be an essential and well-planned part of the room's design. Somehow space has to be found for all or some of the following: clothes, shoes, underclothes, hats, make-up, jewelry, accessories of every description, and an extraordinary amount of impedimenta that always seems to end up in the bedroom. In an ideal world we would each have a walk-in closet with room for everything and everything in its place. This closet—or closets—would have been fitted out in a small room, or rooms, *next* to the master bedroom, as opposed to chopping off a valuable part of that room. There would also be somewhere convenient for a large bureau to take all personal papers, as well as shelves for books.

Alas, this is not an ideal world, and although some of us have the space for such useful planning, most of us have not. All the same, if you really set your mind to it and consider all the possibilities, you can sometimes work

small miracles. Clearly, it is not possible to give any sort of blueprint on storage that will suit everyone, but there are certain common sense methods for better organizing whatever space you do have at your disposal. And incidentally, *would* it be possible to lop off a bit of the room to make a walk-in closet without spoiling the proportions? Sometimes it is. Or you can take a bit from your room and a bit from the room next door without really spoiling either. It's worth a thought and a try.

FITTING IT ALL IN

Whether storage is to be custom-built, bought ready-made, or somehow improvised, it must be fitted into the room as neatly and inconspicuously as possible. Otherwise, the most elegant of furnishings and decoration will be spoilt by the undisciplined welter of belongings. I am not referring here to freestanding pieces like armoires, fitted wardrobes, bureaus, and chests of drawers, because those have an integrity in their own right, but rather to the somewhat higgledy-piggledy patchwork of closets and drawer storage that some people manage to amass.

If you are planning a room from scratch and it lacks any previously built-in closets, you should take particular note of your room's proportions and architectural details. In an old building, bedrooms with high ceilings and nice moldings might be best served with a freestanding armoire. Large, old pieces can often be bought inexpensively and can usually be refinished or painted—if they are particularly shabby—and reorganized inside to take a good many possessions.

If you decide on built-in storage, or built-in *looking* storage (because most new storage units are modular and can be made to look custom-built), take a note of any convenient recesses, or a spare wall or corner. A wall that has a door or doors in it could have closets built *around* the door or doors so that you seem to walk through deep closets into the room, or to the landing or bathroom beyond. This is often a very good way of getting extra storage without encroaching upon room space. The same thing could be done for a window wall, especially if you can incorporate a dressing table and drawers as well.

Try to ensure that all cupboards reach ceiling height and that any moldings or baseboards that are covered are re-introduced and matched along the fronts. Few things spoil the proportions of a room so much as an unsightly gap between the top of a closet and the ceiling, quite apart from the fact that it is a waste of space and a dust trap. Even if ceilings are tall so that the top cupboards are then

LEFT: A row of different-colored baskets provide decorative storage for a mass of small things under the basin area off a spacious bedroom. Wicker baskets underneath hold linens, while tiered small baskets behind the recessed shelves above are just as useful. Note the shelves of shoes to the left.

OPPOSITE: A whole armoire full of hats becomes a highly decorative thing in its own right.

very high, you can put away your least used objects up there and reach them, when necessary, with a step ladder.

To be really unobtrusive, any sort of closet fronts should be made to seem part of the walls and brought in with the same decorative treatment whether painted, wallpapered, or fabric-covered. If wallpapered, the paper should be taken inside the doors as well and the whole given a couple of coats of matte or eggshell polyurethane to prevent the paper tearing and wearing. Or the paper could be brought to the edge of the doors and then covered with a thin beading. Of course, if closets are good-looking in their own right, they do not have to be unobtrusive.

ORGANIZING THE INTERIORS

Whether you are building new storage or trying to reorganize the storage you already have, there are certain pointers to using the space to its best advantage:

- Clothes racks are often unnecessarily high so that the space below is not properly utilized. A reasonable

height is 5 feet (1.5m) from the bottom of the closet, leaving the top part free for generous shelving space. Alternatively, you can have two banks of rods for short clothes like shirts, jackets, and trousers in one closet (or part of a closet), and longer hanging space for coats, evening clothes, and so on, in another. Always try to fit in generous shoe racks.

- If there are few drawers in a room but many shelves, wire or cane baskets are a good idea for keeping underclothes, folded shirts, sweaters, socks, and similar items tidy. Stacking plastic drawers or trays can be fitted into a suitable place; they are especially good in clear plastic so that you can see the contents at a glance. Tie, belt, and scarf racks can be fixed to the insides of doors.

- Do not forget that valuable space under the bed. Drawers here can take winter sweaters or duvets in the summer, T-shirts and left-over summer things in the winter, and, of course, it's a great area for stashing luggage.

Bathrooms

WASHING FACILITIES SEEM TO HAVE COME LAST on the list of household necessities for alarmingly long periods in the history of Western Civilization. An Englishman complained of his Oxford College in the 1950s that it denied him the everyday facilities of Minoan Crete. And indeed Minoan skill in sanitary engineering appears to have far surpassed that of the Chileans, Egyptians, and Greeks (I leave out the Romans, who were good while they lasted), who were all in turn far superior to the Anglo-Saxons who had hardly a bathroom in the kingdom after the 300-year Roman occupation (although the Romans left a sophisticated network of public baths, plumbing systems, and aqueducts) until the late seventeenth century. The Queen's bathroom in King Minos' Palace at Knossos, unearthed by Sir Arthur Evans in the early part of the twentieth century, was as sumptuous a room as any contemporary bathroom. It included an ergonomically satisfying and beautifully decorated bathtub. Even the toilet facilities were curiously modern. One of them evidently had a wooden seat and probably an earthenware pan as well as a reservoir for flushing water.

A swing-arm lamp is reflected into the mirror in this prettily wallpapered bathroom with its collection of gilt-framed paintings.

Although not quite so talented at plumbing, the ancient Greeks, at least if you believe Homer, always seemed to have good hot baths to return to after their interminable travels. According to Lawrence Wright's *Clean and Decent* (Routledge & Paul, 1960), that invaluable history of the bath, fourth-century Rome had eleven public baths, one thousand and fifty-two fountains and cisterns, and eight hundred and fifty-six private baths. Some private houses in Pompeii are believed to have had as many as thirty taps, in addition to private flushing toilets (there were plenty of public ones as well).

Although in most of Europe it was more normal to go largely unwashed than washed for centuries, there was a major exception: medieval monasteries set a shining example for cleanliness. At Canterbury in Kent, a complete water service was installed in the monastery in 1150. It must have been efficient; that particular monastery was one of the few communities to escape the Black Death in 1349. Many ruined monasteries display sociable rows of pierced stone seats sometimes back to back, with a small division between each, though occasionally they were arranged in a circle. Their bath houses had plain round or oval wooden tubs made of oak or walnut.

A curved wooden platform made from old wood makes an island of this bath in a sea of black and white tiles. A pot of geraniums makes another demarcation line.

Medieval books of etiquette insisted upon the washing of hands, face, and teeth every morning, and the washing of hands before and after meals (which was only practical considering that people ate with their fingers); but they made no particular mention of bathing, though baths certainly existed, and were at least offered to travelers when they first arrived. Since there were no pipes, hot water was scarce, so whole families and their guests would bathe together, which was presumably more sociable than sanitary. There is a fascinating late-fifteenth-century woodcut showing a bathhouse cum bordello where a minstrel is playing to couples seated on either side of a long wooden bath with a centerboard full of food, plates, and mugs, and a man at the far end is "washing" a woman's legs. In addition, restorations of medieval castles and chateaux show that at this time there were also portable wooden tubs designed for one person. Sometimes, according to medieval illustrations, the entire bath was enveloped in a tent of fabric, more for the steam this engendered than the privacy.

While the sixteenth-century Italian Popes and nobles had sumptuous bathrooms with frescoed walls, marble baths, and hot and cold water taps; and while Leonardo da Vinci was devising hot water systems providing premixed bath water, three parts hot and one part cold, and facilities with flushing channels and ventilating shafts, the British made no significant sanitary progress and stuck to their chamber pots and "close-stools" or "stools of ease." These were box-like stools with padded seats, sometimes decorated with velvet, leather, or elaborate painting and kept either in the sleeping quarters or just outside. It is true that in the 1590s, a century after Leonardo da Vinci, a Sir John Harrington designed a lavatory complete with seat, pan, cistern, overflow pipe, and flushing system. But although the Queen had one built in her palace at Richmond, just outside London, the invention did not come into general use until it was reinvented again some two hundred years later.

The bathroom here was installed in an old bedroom, as can be seen by the beamed ceiling above the two arched recesses for shower and lavatory. The centrally placed bath between the two is an elegant idea—it looks very white in the middle of all the mellowness.

In the seventeenth century, the contents of chamber pots and "closed stools" all over the British Isles were tipped out of countless windows onto the streets below to the accompaniment of warning cries of "Gardy-loo," derived in the Anglo-French cross culture from *"Gardez-L'eau"* (mind the water). In France, superior versions of the closed stool that could be flushed were called *"Lieux a l'Anglais"* (English places), the derivation of the modern English "loo," like the American "John." In grand homes of the seventeenth century, baths of alabaster and marble were introduced. In lesser houses, the servants brought in copper baths and placed them in front of the bedchamber fire. In farms and small town and country houses and cottages, this ritual was more likely to take place in a tin bath in front of the kitchen range.

During the eighteenth century, bathrooms in large country houses became more common with the addition of plunge baths and primitive showers. In 1730, the Duke of Marlborough had his own bathroom at Blenheim Palace placed outside his library for all to see, with bowl, tub, floors, and walls in marble. At Woburn, in 1748, the Duke of Bedford installed a drainage system, complete with four

facilities, "at least one within the house." Yet, even as late as 1760, fixed bathrooms were still very rare indeed.

In the 1780s, lavatories fitted with valves became available for the first time since Sir John Harrington's Elizabethan era invention. A watchmaker, Alexander Cummings, had taken out a patent in 1775, but the valve was unreliable. Joseph Bramah, a cabinetmaker, patented a greatly improved model in 1778 and produced six thousand in his first year. The company went on making them to the same pattern until 1890, many exported to the United States.

In the nineteenth century, sanitary arrangements gradually improved. Washstands began to be available to the general public, as did basins and bidets, and shaving tables were built with integral mirrors. Decorated china basins and pitchers or jugs for washing, which were placed on a washstand, were now quite commonplace. Alas, even when running water became ubiquitous and its regular use accepted, it was seldom piped above the basement. Thus servants had to run up and down the stairs with jugs of water, and basins and baths mostly remained portable affairs in a great many ingenious shapes.

By the 1880s, more and more people began turning spare bedrooms into bathrooms, though taps with hot and cold water were still rare. Americans, however, took to the new

This bathroom is another tribute to the Napoleonic Campaigns. Wide marble stripes in the bath recess, the deep bath, even Napoleon's bees on the tied-back and fringed bath curtains, not to mention the swan neck faucets, are all nods to the early-nineteenth-century influence. The arched mirror at the back of the recess helps to exaggerate the given space.

plumbing industry with enthusiasm and were soon known to Europeans as "the most tubbed and scrubbed people on earth." Although at first most domestic bathrooms were very much bedrooms which happened to have sanitary appliances moved in, newly custom-built early-twentieth-century bathrooms were often very stylish. Art Deco bathrooms had marble floors, lacquered walls, stainless steel-framed mirrors, washstands on stainless steel legs, with sometimes some sort of screen shielding the lavatory. However, through most of the 1920s onwards in American cities, new bathrooms were often clinically tiled boxes or slits of rooms, with a shower over the bath and not much room for decoration.

For the last twenty-five years or so, many bathrooms have become a kind of status symbol, with larger houses and apartments having his and hers en suite bathrooms decorated as personally as their owners desired. This is a long shot indeed from so many family bathrooms with their collection of bath toys, soggy towels, moldering shower curtains, limp fragments of soap, puddled floors, and toothpaste-splashed mirrors. Personally, I like bathrooms with collections of this and that, plants, prints, and photographs, and efficient appliances, masses of hot water, good storage for make-up, spare soaps, toothbrushes and toothpastes, toilet necessities and medicines, with really excellent lighting and *heated* towel rails. (Why don't generally efficient American bathrooms have these as standard, I wonder?) And if I could really have my way, I would have a working fireplace, too.

This room aspires to the grandeur of a nineteenth-century boudoir-like bathroom, with its grand mirror, gilded chair and claw feet, not to mention the gilded heated towel rail behind the bath.

Powder Rooms

THE AMERICAN "POWDER ROOM" SEEMS a much more logical term to use for that useful little room than the British "cloakroom," which must be as outdated a word, as, for example, the "wireless." As it is generally small, it lends itself to fairly fanciful decoration, as much for the lack of expense entailed in such a small area as for the fun. The romantic version has them with mahogany paneling, converted etched glass oil or gas lamps, generous mirrors, and an air of opulent comfort left over from the Edwardian era. This is a far cry from the cold, damp, unwelcoming space that was the favored European treatment from the 1920s to the 1960s, or thereabouts. The Americans did much better, adding a certain amount of Hollywood glamour, but it is only in the last forty years or so that the powder room has really come into its own.

In fact, the lighting, floors, and windows in powder rooms can follow much the same criteria as bathrooms, but they should also be as thoughtfully accessorized as guest bedrooms, with special soap, nice hand towels (old ones are always good here), a spare clean brush and comb for those who have forgotten theirs, and maybe the odd lipstick and powder for equally forgetful women. A spare electric razor, or an old fashioned razor and shaving soap, might not go amiss either, and these various accoutrements presuppose a cabinet or corner cupboard of some decorative sort, or a small cupboard built into the wall or concealed behind the mirror. When guests are around, it would be pleasant to include a glass or two and a bottle of mineral water or carafe of fresh water.

A mixture of tortoiseshell faux painted paneling, mirror, marble, battened fabric—the same as the Roman shade—flowers, and scent bottles give this powder room a nostalgic Edwardian feel.

Decorative Options

In bathrooms, you can create a sense of quiet luxury with discreet but beautiful materials: a beautifully detailed mirror and lighting; beautifully designed hardware; thick plate-glass shower stalls with no evidence of hinges to rust; marble, limestone, or granite floors, sometimes inlaid; marble, granite, or limestone sink counters; and bathtub sides with generous rims around them for soaps, bath oils and essences, sweet-smelling candles, and colognes and toilet waters.

Walls

Practicality, a sense of quality, and common sense come first in bathrooms, with whatever you fancy next. Alternatively, powder rooms can pretty well be as fanciful as preferred. For example, you could have extravagantly battened old paisley fabric walls in a powder room, or any other fabric that looks handsome, while fabric in a bathroom is likely to get soaked or dampened with steam. Any sort of tile paint finish is also good here, as is tongue and groove wood. A deep lacquer looks distinguished in a powder room, as does paneling or faux paneling, or a paneled dado with an interesting finish or wallpaper above.

This, too, can look really good in a bathroom used by careful people, especially if it is mahogany, or mahoganized, with a countertop to match. (The counter top will need to be sealed well with varnish for protection from splashes.) A powder room, by the way, can use really expensive wallpaper without breaking the bank. If you use wallpaper in the bathroom it needs to be given a coat or two of protective clear varnish or polyurethane. Right now, there is a trend for glass walls and partitions, which can be clear or smoked, etched, or maybe glass bricks.

Lighting

Since most bathrooms and powder rooms are small, one can often get away with good lighting over or at the sides of the mirror above the basin. As always, Hollywood strips give the best light for make-up repairs and shaving, though good bright wall lamps set at either side of the mirror are efficient too, as long as they reflect light onto the face. If the room is a little larger, ceiling light would be in order, preferably recessed down-lights, or if that is not possible, specially-sealed bathroom ceiling fixtures, which can also be fixed over the shower or bathtub.

An all marble bathroom with raised sinks and a huge walk-in shower, is made even more sumptuous with the Oriental rugs and mahogany paneled doors. It is not so very different in feeling from the immensely luxurious Italian sixteenth-century papal and noble bathrooms.

Flooring

In a family or beach house bathroom, non-slip ceramic tile or terrazzo is definitely the cheapest and most practical. Marble, granite, and limestone are satisfyingly elegant in both bathrooms and powder rooms. Synthetic fiber carpet is comfortable in both rooms, being easy to clean and quicker to dry than wool. Polished wood and a small Oriental rug or kelim are good in a powder room not too much frequented by children, and likewise in such a bathroom. Painted or stenciled wood floors are good for both rooms, especially in the country or by the shore. The various mattings are a bit hard on bare feet, but they look good and again can be teamed with a rug or two.

Choose from:
- Non-slip ceramic floor tiles
- Marble, granite, or limestone
- Wood (natural or painted)
- Man-made fiber carpet (easy to clean and quick to dry)
- Coir, sisal, sea grass, or rush matting

Windows

Many bathrooms do not have windows, but most powder rooms seem to have at least small ones. If bathroom windows are far enough away from the bathtub, they can be treated quite normally with curtains—if they do not get in the way— or shades of some sort, shutters, or screens. Another treatment is to simply mount glass shelves across them, filled with plants, a collection of colored glass, or a mixture. Stained glass can be extremely attractive in either room.

LEFT: The claw-footed, whimsically-painted bathtub in this large room stands on a "rug" of marble inset into a carpeted floor. This provides the best of both worlds for feet both wet and dry.

ABOVE: Shuttered windows, a vase full of wild flowers, and a patterned blue and white basin in a shallow sink are all simple and nice ideas that add up to a charming room.

Furnishings

Unless you have a really spacious room, neither bathroom nor powder room can take much furniture, and anything to do with storage should take priority. You will need to take maximum advantage of the space under the basin or basins, and behind and around any mirror, so you can stash away all the soaps, bath oils, make-up, shaving supplies, medicines, and cleaning necessities. Any furniture, therefore, is really in the nature of a bonus. First, the necessities: a shower/bathtub/basin(s), lavatory, and bidet (depending upon space); a good mirror or mirrors; maximum storage, including drawers, shelves, and cabinets; and a chair or stool. If you can fit in any of the following, so much the better: a comfortable chair; a dressing table and chair; a small chest of drawers; and a small table and bookcase.

Accessories

Both bathrooms and powder rooms are excellent repositories for odd collections of this and that which might look somewhat flippant in any other room, so it is useful to put shelves up where you can. Bathrooms are also nurturing places for most plants. Both rooms lend themselves to purely cosmetic decoration, which can hide a multitude of sins. Old tiles in a displeasing color can be painted with a good oil or special tile paint. Old baths and basins can be painted with special bathroom appliance paint. Boring, dark little spaces can be glamorized with collections of old prints or photographs. If there is room, it is nice to add a small table with nice-smelling things, tissues, magazines, scented candles, or whatever you prefer.

LEFT TOP: What this room lacks in size it makes up for with its collection of very varied art and mirrors, and comfortable warm towels from the heated towel rail. The cluttered walls are a good antidote to the freestanding tub.

LEFT BOTTOM: Apothecary jars filled with shells and stones, a group of carvings, and a large brass door knocker adorn the pale terra-cotta walls in this semi-paneled room. Note the bamboo beading just below the marble-topped shelf, and the shell-edged frame just seen to the left of the photograph.

OPPOSITE: One of the advantages of turning a previous bedroom into a bathroom in an old house is the possibility of getting a bonus fireplace. This one is especially grand with a mahogany overmantel to boot. To this dominant feature has been added mahogany bath panels and a mahogany dressing table and mirror. Note the graceful little chair and framed gouaches on sludgy green mattes.

Children's Rooms

THE VAST MAJORITY OF CHILDREN'S ROOMS, whether bedroom or playroom or both, have to be able to grow with the child. This does not mean that you cannot go to town on the decorations. On the contrary, you can be as imaginative and colorful as you like as long as the basics are in place.

A Room to Grow

IT IS A FACT THAT ALMOST EVERYONE EXPECTING their first child who has the wherewithal, will start to think nostalgically when planning their child's room. Anyone with experience will start to think more practically. The good old-fashioned nursery with its guarded fire; the old rocking chair; the white-painted iron crib that can be gently rocked; the pastel colors and tiny prints or dazzling white muslins—these elements are still in most first-time parents' minds when they start to plan. And most of these harbored nostalgic ideas were inspired by fairly prosperous Victorian or Edwardian family life.

Before the Victorian age, children hardly entered into the planning of a house; they were just fitted in wherever it seemed convenient, not unlike the majority of families today. But in the prosperous nineteenth century, the Victorian concept of a large united family meant that children were placed on their own nursery floor, within tolerably easy reach of their parents, and very much within reach of their nanny, if not an under-nanny as well. There is a charming recollection of Marjorie Strachey's in *Two Victorian Families* by Betty Askwith (1971): "Mama used to wear a little gold bell on her watch chain. The nursery was right at the top of a very high house, and the inhabitants were likely to feel lonely and cut off from the rest of the world. Suddenly one would hear the tinkling of the gold bell coming nearer and nearer. I shall never forget the exciting anticipation of interest and pleasure that came with it."

The truth of the matter is that the vast majority of children's rooms—whether they are combined sleeping cum playrooms (which is the norm), or just bedrooms

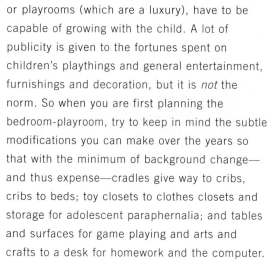

or playrooms (which are a luxury), have to be capable of growing with the child. A lot of publicity is given to the fortunes spent on children's playthings and general entertainment, furnishings and decoration, but it is *not* the norm. So when you are first planning the bedroom-playroom, try to keep in mind the subtle modifications you can make over the years so that with the minimum of background change—and thus expense—cradles give way to cribs, cribs to beds; toy closets to clothes closets and storage for adolescent paraphernalia; and tables and surfaces for game playing and arts and crafts to a desk for homework and the computer.

This does not mean that you cannot go to town on the decoration. On the contrary, you can be as imaginative, colorful, and indulgent as you like with accessories, fabrics, storage boxes, bunk beds, and so on. But if the background or framework of the room, the basic furniture, and the storage is simple, sturdy, and classic, you will be able to afford to change certain parts (window treatments, bed sizes, accessories, colors) without structural or expensive alterations.

BELOW: As young girls mature, their preferences in decoration and furnishings often become increasingly less juvenile and more feminine. Flourishes such as this array of frilled blue and white pillows and cushions could appeal to many a pre-teen and teenage girl.

OPPOSITE: In this charming little girl's room, two delicate, curtained iron four-poster beds are dressed in blue and white toile, trimmed in blue, and teamed with a blue and white rug. A large white-painted chest holds toys and the second bed is for friends who sleep over.

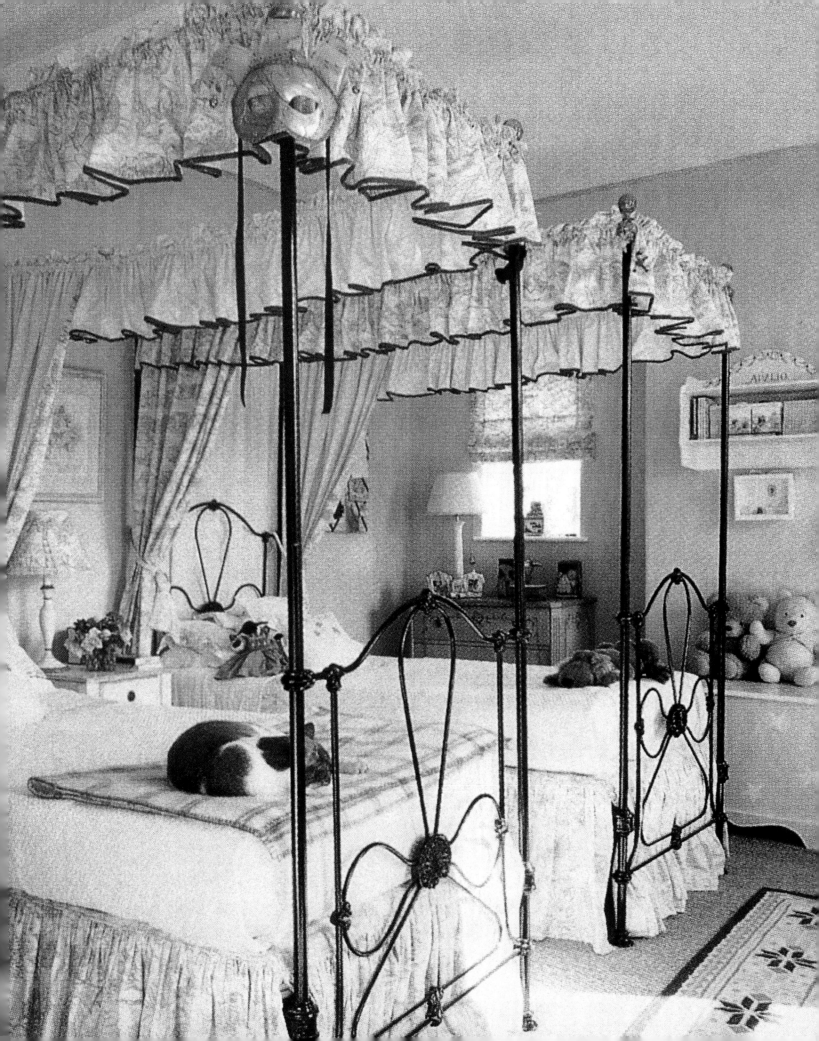

Stacks of transparent plastic boxes provide useful toy storage all along one wall in this child's room. The brightly colored alphabet rug on the large floor area is a terrific idea and provides most of the color in the room, apart, that is, from the toys.

Infants

Many years ago, I evolved a classic formula for "the room that grows with the child." I see no reason, since it seems to work, not to use it again. Of course it can be embellished as and when you can afford it, or when you are given things, and certainly children themselves will soon want a say, but this is a good framework to follow, not necessarily slavishly, but as a basis for thought.

For the infant's room, I painted the walls white and put down a vinyl-coated cork tile floor for quietness and practicality. (I could just as easily have kept to wood or put down an inexpensive carpet.) I added a large, colorful cotton rug (easily washable) on top. I put up a Venetian shade, which meant that the light could easily be varied for daytime naps or early mornings. (I thought curtains could all too easily be pulled when the infant started to crawl and walk.) I prettied up an old family rocking crib or cradle with machine washable Broderie Anglaise—a lovely combination of pierced openwork with raised white embroidery. I built in a full-size closet with a stack of shelves on one side and a double row of hanging rods on the other. At this stage the shelves were scheduled to hold soft toys, spare diapers, and foldable clothes.

I bought a pair of good-sized unfinished wood chests of drawers, placed them against the wall with a knee hole in between, painted them white and put a white laminate top (easy to wipe down) over the two, which I then had secured. This provided a lot more storage as well as a changing surface. I also bought a two-tiered cart, which could be easily wheeled around, to hold the plastic bath, diapers, towels, talcum powder, wipes, and all the rest of the infant's toilet and dressing requirements.

Final touches were a rocking chair for nursing, an old club chair, a few pictures, a wallpaper ceiling border, and recessed lights on a dimmer switch. These lights were strategically placed over the changing area and near the crib and could be dimmed down for minimum disturbance and maximum reassurance at night. A corkboard was added behind the chests of drawers to pin up weight charts, pediatrician appointments, and various reminders.

Toddlers and Preschoolers

At this point in the room's evolution, the cradle was put aside and a crib introduced. This had to be both safe and sturdy, which meant making sure that the slats were not more than $2^3/8$ inches (6cm) apart, that the rails were an adequate height for protection even when the drop side was lowered, that the drop sides themselves were the sort that could not be released by the child, and that the mattress was a perfect fit with no dangerous gaps left at the sides.

The window treatment was left the same. An old wooden chest was imported to cater to the overflow of toys (but any chest or toy crate will do). All of the baby accessories that were no longer needed were put away, but the cart was left as a useful space for storing games (it was too heavy to be pushed around by a toddler). At this stage I also invested in a little carpentry work: I had some bookshelves made on one of the walls because the piles of books were becoming unmanageable. Also, as the room got very hot in the summer, I had some reasonably close-together vertical bars clamped into a frame screwed into the sides of the window so that there would be no possibility of youthful explorations onto the outside sill when the window was opened up. To make sure it was not prison-like, the bars were painted alternating bright colors. The corkboard was used for pinning up first drawings and paintings, as well as for various reminders of dates and such. The walls were still able to be kept fairly pristine in spite of the ravages of dirty little hands and scribbles, because white paint is so easy to touch up. Still, just to encourage drawings in the right place, I added a large blackboard and secured it against the wall from the floor for easy access.

As children grow from infant to toddler, so their accumulation of toys, games, and art supplies seem to expand. Storage in children's bedrooms and playrooms should be attractive and neat, and should allow for safe and easy access for little hands.

Grade Schoolers

As the child approached school age, the crib went out and was replaced by a couple of modular bunk beds (though a single twin bed would be fine, or even better, one with a trundle bed underneath). The bunk beds were useful in a variety of ways since they were the kind that could be dismantled and turned into two ordinary beds and also had an extra large drawer underneath for even more toy and game storage. Although the room was for one child, bunk beds were a good investment as they meant there was always room for a friend to stay overnight and they provided a play area at different levels. It was now safe to take down the window bars, and I changed the Venetian shade for a fabric Roman variety.

A couple of chairs and an angled desk light were added so the laminated chests of drawers could now be used as a desk for homework as well as for painting, model-making, and so on. Large flat books, drawing and painting paper, and paints and crayons were kept in the top drawers, underclothes and similar in the bottom. The pin-board went on being practical and the shelves in the closet were now used for sweaters, shorts, and T-shirts, as well as toys. The cart became useful for storing jigsaw puzzles and other games on its lower level, and for a small television on top. The walls were adorned with more and more drawings, paintings, and other memorabilia with just enough space left for a mirror.

As the child went from elementary to grade school, the bunk beds came down and turned into two couch-like beds placed at right angles, with tailored covers, cushions, and an extra long drawer under what was the top bunk. The major purchases at this stage were

Cut out panels of wallpaper, and strips of the same paper used to surround pictures, are only one of the clever ideas in this child's room. A white-painted chair is over-painted with small pink hearts to match the pink stripes and picture frame; the headboard is upholstered in the same stripes as the curtains and bed frill, and there is a long surface, just seen in the foreground, for drawing, playing, and homework.

a new rug and a shade to go with the new bedcovers, a secondhand computer to go on the laminated top, and a low wooden table to go between the beds with a bedside lamp. There was no longer any need for the blackboard. The ladder for the bunk beds was painted bright yellow and hung on the wall like a piece of sculpture along with the posters. The pin-board began to be used for posting school events as well as reminders. The wallpaper border was removed and replaced with a new one.

Teenagers

As the child grew into her teenage years, I wallpapered the walls with her cooperation and input. (This particular bedroom beloned to a girl, but that does not preclude doing the same thing for a boy to suit *his* tastes.) I curtained the window, leaving the shade underneath since the color was still fine. This go round I put carpet on the floor for a softer look. The rocking chair was given a coat of paint and the old club chair was re-covered. I changed the bedcovers and cushions. The pin-board was taken down and replaced with more pictures and prints. The bookshelves, closet, and chests of drawers stayed the same except for a coat of paint and the inevitable change of contents. By adding a table mirror the laminated top became a dressing table at one end as well as a desk. A stereo was placed on top, with racks for CDs and tapes, and still there was enough room to work. The old cart was repainted and remained a television stand with a DVD player underneath. The old wooden toy chest was stenciled and became a coffee table in front of one of the couch-like beds. The room by now had assumed a totally different character, but it had by no means been a costly metamorphosis, just a very gradual one and affordable at every stage. Obviously this is just one way of doing a child's room, but it has stood the test of time well enough, which is really what classic home decorating is about.

Matching duvets and pillowcovers on the bunk beds are teamed with a witch-patterned rug in this highly practical room. The gray wall conceals a whole range of cupboards and wide, deep drawers for all the children's toys and clothing. Note the design of the beds with their integral ladder at one end, and small built-in wood tables by the pillow ends for clocks, radios, and books.

Decorative Options

While there are numerous practical considerations in designing children's rooms, they should not preclude fun and imagination. After all, it is a *child's* room, and should ideally appeal to and stimulate young minds. Nevertheless, safety should always come first, and outlets, windows, and all other such hazards should be diligently secured.

Walls

When a child is small you will want walls that can be wiped or washed easily, in a color that can be touched up. If you have set your heart on pretty wallpaper, make a dado at waist height and paint below; this way you can keep the room looking fairly pristine until the child is old enough not to smudge and scribble all over the place. Wallpaper borders will add interest to plain walls, or you can get contact-backed paper motifs that can be easily peeled off and changed. If you do make a dado, you can also cover it with transfers like a Victorian patch screen, or with old magazine pictures carefully layered with varnish to make it both washable and long lasting. Another idea with white or pale walls is to paint large rainbows, trees, or what you like. They can be painted over easily as the child grows and changes.

Lighting

It is not a good idea to have table lamps in a very small child's room, unless you need one for extra light; it is all too easy for a small child to pull at cords and topple a lamp. Otherwise, whatever you choose for ambient light should be on a dimmer switch or switches (so that one light can be left on at night and dimmed down if the child is afraid of the dark). If a child is really frightened and you cannot dim the light down far enough, you can get a small nightlight, and supplement it if necessary with a corridor light dimmed down outside the door. As the child gets older, he or she will need a light for reading, doing homework, and so on, so desk and bedside lights are in order. Do be sure to get caps to cover all exposed outlets once the child is at the crawling stage.

Flooring

In an apartment you might need to have carpet to deaden the sound, although cork and vinyl, and plain vinyl are reasonably soft and soundproof, and are also easy on the knees when crawling. You can soften these floors with a cotton rug or two if you like. If you have nice wood floors, or painted wood floors, make sure there are no rough parts to provide splinters, and add a rug or two as well. Sand rough areas smooth with fine-grade sandpaper and wipe the surface with a soft cloth. Then paint or varnish to seal the wood and to blend it with the surrounding floor area. Top with a rug or two, for safety making sure that all rugs are non-slip and well-secured.

> **Choose between:**
> - Carpet
> - Wood or painted wood and a rug
> - Vinyl or vinyl mix and a rug (preferably cotton for easy washing)

Windows

Make sure that windows are stopped or barred in some way to prevent adventurous children from climbing out. Curtains, unless they are short, are not a good idea for toddlers, who will tug at them, or trip on them. You will usually need some sort of shade or shutters that won't let in light in the morning and can be drawn for daytime naps. Venetian shades or any of the excellent ready-made shades on the market would be good and you can change them or dress them up with curtains later on.

Furnishings

As far as furnishings, you will need at minimum: a cradle, crib, or bed of some sort; a chair; a closet; a chest of drawers (with a top deep enough to change the baby); and storage containers and shelves for toys. As the child grows, you may want at least one other chest of drawers so you can make a desk area, or a desk and desk chair. Bonus furnishings could include a club or armchair, a chest for toys, a cart, and a bedside and side table. Of course, when a child is tiny, you could always have your chest of drawers perform double-duty as a crib by doing as Oliver Goldsmith (1730?-74) wrote of a humbler room:

> The white-wash'd wall, the nicely sanded floor,
> The varnish'd clock that click'd behind the door.
> The chest contriv'd a double debt to pay,
> A bed at night, a chest of drawers by day...

Accessories

Once safety and practical considerations are taken care of, rooms for small children can be as magical and as colorful as you can make them. Dollhouses, stuffed animals, toy trains, building blocks, games, books, and dressing-up clothes...all the ingredients in fact, to excite a young mind. Decorate walls with images of fanciful creatures, castles, pirate ships, childhood heroes, or bright alphabet letters, numbers, and other painless aids to learning. Wooden boxes or laundry hampers make excellent toy storage. As children mature, they will increasingly want a say in how their rooms look and feel, as well as what they want. However much their ideas collide with yours, it is important to allow school age children some involvement in their room's progression, for this is how they will develop confidence in their own style.

Shelves full of hampers in bright, primary colors overflow with toys and make cheap and practical children's room storage. In this case, they also provide a good deal of the decoration, along with the transfers on the wall. Note the beige-colored rug edged with red.

Safety First

Small children like to explore. Secure your home with safety supplies designed to take the worry out of childcare. In addition to electrical outlet caps, there are cord shorteners to help keep dangling cords out of reach. Furnishings should be outfitted with drawer and cabinet latches, and sharp table edges should be cushioned with corner protectors. In the kitchen, deter young explorers with appliance latches and stovetop shields, which protect small hands from hot burners and pans. Block stairs with adjustable gates, and shield stair, porch, and balcony railings with rail-nets. Try not to make it too easy for children to climb.

Porches, Loggias, Terraces, and Verandahs

WHETHER YOU CALL IT A CONSERVATORY, PORCH,
loggia, terrace (or *terrasse* as the French say), or verandah,
it is all the same thing in different guises in different countries:
in other words, an invaluable indoor/outdoor summer living room.

Outdoor Living Rooms

THE PORCH IS AN AMERICAN INSTITUTION, from the deep South where so many houses display them right out front, if not all around, to the Finger Lakes, from Maine to California, there they are lording it out in the sun in cities, towns, villages, in the country and by the beach. The very name evokes immediate thoughts of slightly peeling clapboard, a charming balustrade overlooking the heat-hazed garden (or the heat-hazed street); and old sofas, wicker chairs, rocking chairs, and gliders casually dispersed around the floor, all intermittently screened by hanging plants, geraniums, and roses. Americans are out on their porches from sweet-smelling sunlit breakfasts to candlelit suppers, with the crickets and tree frogs drowning the conversation. The American porch is essentially laid-back; the epitome of long, languorous summer days, iced teas, mint juleps, and ice cold glasses of wine. Somehow or other "the deck" does not have quite the same resonance as "the porch."

Loggias sound more Italian, more South of France, somehow more deliberately glamorous perhaps, with their smart lounging furniture and massed pots of bougainvillea or oleander, clipped urns of box and privet; sometimes half indoors, half outdoors, sometimes right outside. Terraces are usually an outdoor adjunct to a drawing room or living room, with or

A long colonial bench is covered in red and black check cushions on this stone porch. The fabric acts as a colorful foil to the stone walls and floor. Hanging lamps over the bench give a mellow light at night.

without a balustrade, with or without a vine-strung pergola, but always with the flowering pots, the table, chairs, and outdoor chaise lounges; though a *terrasse* in France, often half-roofed or under a *tonnelle* or pergola, can lead off any room—kitchen, living room, bedroom—in any sort of house.

Verandah is an old Hindi name for a pillared porch, the kind of seductive, elegant lounging space found all over India, South America, Africa, Egypt, The East and West Indies, Australia, New Zealand, Fiji, the East in general, not to mention the Middle East, Turkey, the Philippines, and on and on. British Colonial workers returning "home" to the United Kingdom after a lifetime spent in the old colonies, built them onto houses in the unsuitable British weather to remind them, one supposes, of the good old days. The idea so enraptured the mainly sun-starved British in the nineteenth century that verandahs were built all over the place, particularly in those places favored by returning travelers.

But what has always been much more sensible for the British, the more northern Europeans, Americans, and, I suppose, most big city dwellers (where the noise and the dust would preclude complete porch enjoyment), or for anyone with less than reliable summer weather, is the glassed-in conservatory with its often intoxicating smells of jasmine and damp foliage, lilies, and gardenias, and great massed ferns and palms. After 1845, when the window or glass tax was repealed in Britain, conservatories leading off drawing rooms or libraries became very popular, not only for the long summer days and evenings,

This porch, almost like a theatre or film set, with its arched trelliswork and low white walls, white floor, furniture, and green stained chairs, looks cool and beautiful for hot summer days and warm, scented nights.

but for the better days of winter as well. Lady Bromley Davenport in her *History of Capesthorne* (1974) reminisces about the conservatory there: "In a magical world of Chinese lanterns, exotic flowers, and intoxicating scents, they sipped their wine and laughed and talked, protected by the fragile glass from the cruelty of the winter's night."

Many Americans screen their porches with fly screens in summer and glass screens in the winter, to achieve much the same effect as a conservatory, much like the nineteenth-century "Winter Gardens" with their jungly plants, blue and white porcelain, and endless cane furniture. I went to school in the house that Napoleon the Third and his wife, Empress Eugene, had as their exile home in England. I spent hours reading in the Winter Garden there absorbing the warm, damp smell of well-watered exotic plants, including the massive clump of pampas grass on which their son, the Prince Imperial, was supposed to have died, speared to death in the Zulu war.

Those heady summer nights seem to have spawned countless soulful moments in many such exotic adjuncts to living rooms. Henry James, Edith Wharton, Anthony Trollope, Willa Cather, Somerset Maugham, et al, used them so often as backgrounds: how many conversations overheard or misunderstood behind the screens of the potted palms? How many evenings spent rocking and ruminating on the porch? How many nervous proposals finally uttered and life's nicest moments blissfully passed?

ABOVE: Pale lilac is not necessarily a color one would think of, but it looks wonderfully cool on this arched loggia with its stone bench covered with striped pillows. Note the pool and fountain in the foreground.

RIGHT: Tawny stone arches look wonderful with the bougainvillea and scattered petals on the marble floor on yet another seductive verandah. The fragility of the foliage in the pots sets off the solidity of the stonework.

OPPOSITE: Deep blue curved walls edged with rose define this unusual loggia. Pale blue lounging chairs reflect the blue of the sky, hills, and sea.

Decorative Options

On the whole, such outdoor spaces furnish themselves. Just as "books do furnish a room," so plants and casual seating decorate a conservatory, porch, loggia, and verandah. They certainly should not look *decorated* in any way, so that leaves primarily the lighting and the floors to think about.

Lighting

The first rule in outdoor lighting is that there should be absolutely nothing bright; a little light goes a long way at night. Also, since light attracts bugs, it might be better to have oil lamps filled with citronella oil, and citronella candles on tables in any outdoor space, with, if there is a garden, any electricity lighting trees and shrubs beyond.

Conservatories, being enclosed, cause less insect problems. Up-lights set at the bottom of tall plants and indoor trees and in corners are the most romantic, with perhaps long hanging lanterns and candles or oil lamps on tables.

Walls

Walls on porches, loggias, and verandahs are best in soft colors, like antique whites, ochres, rosy pinks, peaches, terra-cottas, and warm pastel shades, that provide cool, reflective surfaces in the hot sun as well as a gentle backdrop to a profusion of greenery. Traditional American porches in cooler climates can be colored in darker shades, such as a Colonial red or raw wood board, to blend with a more rustic setting.

Flooring

Clearly, on outdoor spaces, such as verandahs, loggias, terraces, and porches, there should always be a hard floor that can be washed down easily and will withstand any amount of watering and hosing. If a porch is fully or partly covered and seems in need of some extra flooring to make it a room, then sisal or coir might be the best options, as long as it is not likely to get too wet from rain or plants.

Choose from:

- Flagstones
- Non-slip terra-cotta tiles
- Non-slip ceramic tiles
- Marble
- Granite
- Treated or painted wood boards
- Coir or sisal matting

BELOW: Pinstriped curtains make a formal entrance to this charming vaulted conservatory. Note the yellow-edged scalloped pelmet fixed over the filmy voile curtains inside the nice jungly space, and the comfortable cane seating with its white pillows.

OPPOSITE TOP: Adjustable brass wall lamps are fixed to the columns on this large square angled porch. It is so sited that chairs can be positioned to look out in several directions at different views.

OPPOSITE BOTTOM: Some rather Gothic-looking white-painted chairs look handsome against the grayish timber floor and roof of this elegant porch.

Windows

Window treatments in conservatories should be light, easy, and protetctive, yet able to be manipulated enough to filter the sun's glare without casting the room into gloom. Plantation or wooden shades, rattan shades, Venetain shades, fabric shades, or any of the huge Hunter Douglas range, are all practical. Those with a lot of roof glass can go the whole gamut and have electric shades that can be operated at the touch of a button.

Furnishings

Furnishings for outdoor living spaces include: old sofas ("old" for rooms exposed to the elements); daybeds; chaise lounges; garden seats, lounges, gliders, and hammocks; cane, wicker, or basket chairs and tables; small side tables for drinks and serving; and an outdoor table (any table is all right for conservatories) and chairs for dining. As a bonus, a barbecue, whether built-in or freestanding, is nice, as is an outdoor fireplace, or a fireplace or stove in the conservatory, or discreet versions of those tall gas heaters they have in outdoor restaurants or restaurant terraces.

Accessories

As mentioned, there is no need for conservatories, porches, loggias, and verandahs to be particularly decorated. Their natural surroundings—plants, flowers and climbers of every description—decorate the space in much the same ways as books decorate a library or study. Antique lanterns or good modern outdoor lights, storm lamps, sturdy candles in big glass holders, candles, hanging baskets, old olive jars, terra-cotta pots, even the odd piece of sculpture or architectural detail can all be added to the mix. Seats can be softened and brightened with cushions and pillows. And fountains, when appropriate, can add the relaxing trickle of water to the general sense of well-being.

ABOVE: A large dark table and chairs are mixed with cane and look solid and satisfying against the painted wood shutters, peach walls, and the tangle of greenery.

RIGHT: Moroccan arches look shadowy and mysterious in the light projected from high swinging iron lanterns. Note the multi-colored pillows and upholstery against the ancient brickwork.

OPPOSITE: Here a throne-like chair sits majestically against the sea and sky on a dreamy terrace.

Resources

Selected Bibliography

Askwith, Betty. *Two Victorian Families.* London: Chatto & Windus, 1971.

Cassell's Household Guide: being a complete encyclopoedia of domestic and social economy, and forming a guide to every department of practical life. 4 vols. London: Cassell and Co., 1869-71.

Climenson, Emily J. ed. *Passages from The Diaries of Mrs. Philip Lybbe Powys of Hardwick House, Oxon, A.D. 1756 to 1808.* London: Longmans & Co., 1899.

Gilliatt, Mary. *Mary Gilliatt's Interior Design Course.* New York: Watson Guptill Publications, 2001.

Hampton, Mark. *Mark Hampton on Decorating.* New York: Tandom, 1989.

Praz, Mario. *An Illustrated History of Interior Decoration: From Pompeii to Art Nouveau.* London: Thames and Hudson, 1964.

Simond, L. (Louis). *Journal of a tour and residence in Great Britain during the years of l810 and 1811.* New York: Eastburn, Kirk and Co., 1815 (New York: T. and W. Mercer).

Smith, George. *Collection of designs for household furniture and interior Decoration.* London: J. Taylor, 1808.

Soane, Sir John. *Designs in architecture.* London: I. Taylor, 1778.

Ware, Isaac. *A complete body of architecture, adorned with plans and elevations from original designs.* London: Printed for T. Osborne and J. Shipton, J. Hodges, L. Davis, J. Ward, and R. Baldwin, booksellers, 1756.

Wright, Lawrence. *Clean and Decent: The Fascinating History of the Bathroom and Water Closet.* London: Routledge & Paul, 1960.

Suppliers

PAINT, FABRIC & WALLPAPER

Behr
1-800-854-0133, ext 3
www.behrpaint.com

Benjamin Moore & Co.
1-800-344-0400
www.benjaminmoore.com

Farrow & Ball
845-369-4912
www.farrow-ball.com

Fine Paints of Europe
1-800-332-1556
www.fine-paints.com
(Martha Stewart Living Color)

The Glidden Company
1-800-454-3336
www.gliddenpaint.com

Janovic Plaza
1-800-772-4381
www.janovic.com

Martin Senour Paints
1-800-MSP-5270
www.martinsenour.com

Pittsburgh Paints
1-800-441-9695
www.pittsburgpaints.com

Pratt & Lambert
1-800-BUY-PRAT
www.prattandlambert.com

Ralph Lauren Paints
1-800-783-4586
www.paintplus.com

The Sherwin Williams Company
1-800-4-SHERWIN
www.Sherwin-Williams.com

The Silk Trading Co.
1-800-854-0396
www.silktrading.com
(silk and casein paints)

Waverly
1-800-423-5881
www.decoratewaverly.com

HOME FURNISHINGS

ABC Carpet and Home
212-473-3000
www.abchome.com
(antiques, furniture, accessories, linens, lighting, rugs)

Many furnishings, including lights, fabrics, wallpapers, upholstery, carpets, and general furniture are only available through designers. Contact **Decor and You, Inc.** at 800-477-3326 (www.decorandyou.com) to access their nationwide list of designers.

Designer Credits

Anta Design: page 111. M. Antonin: page 96. Monika Apponyi: pages 23, 33, 51, 83, 105, 133, 154. Ruth Aram: page 17, 75, 118. Chateau la Bourdaissiere: pages 64, 108. Joan Brendle: page 119. Jeremy Brooke: pages 54, 84, 92, 102. Anthony Brooks: page 94. Candy & Candy: page 43. Katie Carr-Ellison: pages 73, 158. Lincoln Cato: pages 15, 89. Jane Churchill: page 93. Annie Constantine: pages 116, 141. Charlotte Crosland: page 147. Neisha Crosland: page 41. Isabelle De Borchgrave: page 156. Bernie De Le Cuona: page 132. Juliet De Valero-Wills: pages 2, 47. Amanda Eliasch: page 88. Nick Etherington-Smith: pages 10, 18, 28, 152. Etienne-Martin: pages 27, 125. Claire Farrow: pages 3, 129. Frank Faulkner: pages 114, 117. Anna French: pages 8, 67, 91, 98. Mary Gilliatt: pages 35, 79, 86. Julia Grassick: page 148. Fleur Greeno: pages 22, 109, 135. Jaime Gubbins: page 134. Bodo Hackbarth: pages 50, 97. Claire Hanson: pages 44, 76, 100, 144. Alison Henry: pages 9, 120, 138. Stephanie Hoppen: pages 104, 121, 125. Hudson Featherston Architects: pages 71, 145, 153. Lawrence Isaacson: page 87. Marc Johnson: pages 123, 151, 154, 157. Susanne Katkhuda: pages 7, 36, 66, 113. Thomas Kerr: pages 55, 103. Suzanne Knighton: pages 34, 42, 48. Le Marakech, Hamburg: pages 19, 20. Pauline Mann: pages 14, 21, 60. Jayne McCormack: page 57. Bonnie Morris: pages 12, 30, 82, 128. Penny Morrison: pages 29, 112, 126. Toni Muntaner: pages 124, 135. Mimi O'Connell: pages 110, 122. Sarah Orecchia: page 45. Sabine Pasley-Tyler: page 136. Chris Pearson: page 70. Geoff Player: page 71. Homeira Pour-Heidari: pages 5, 106. Reed/Boyd Design: page 101. Michael Reeves: pages 4, 38. Nico Rensch: page 68, 70, 142. Moussie Sayers: pages 32, 40, 58. John Simpson: pages 4, 7, 15, 24, 56, 131, 155. Inge Sprawson: pages 36, 81. Sophie Stonor: pages 46, 49. Spencer Swaffer: pages 74, 77, 137. Barbara Ther: page 93. William Thuillier: page 26, 32, 61, 85. Gordana Tyler: pages 72, 76, 90, 99. Sarah Vanrenen: pages 1, 115, 137. Konstantin von Haeften: pages 27, 37, 53, 57. Nona von Haeften: pages 130, 152, 59. Tatiana von Hessen: pages 31, 78, 119, 140, 150. Marina von Reuss: page 13. Peter Wadley: pages 34, 62. Dawna Walter: pages 7, 16, 52, 69, 72, 127. Lisa Zahnke: page 6.

Index